FRAUD RISK IN GOVERNMENTAL AND NOT-FOR-PROFIT ORGANIZATIONS

BY LYNDA DENNIS, CPA, CGFO, PH.D.

Notice to Readers

Recognizing and Responding to Fraud Risk in Governmental and Not-for-Profit Organizations is intended solely for use in continuing professional education and not as a reference. It does not represent an official position of the American Institute of Certified Public Accountants, and it is distributed with the understanding that the author and publisher are not rendering legal, accounting, or other professional services in the publication. This course is intended to be an overview of the topics discussed within, and the author has made every attempt to verify the completeness and accuracy of the information herein. However, neither the author nor publisher can guarantee the applicability of the information found herein. If legal advice or other expert assistance is required, the services of a competent professional should be sought.

You can qualify to earn free CPE through our pilot testing program.
If interested, please visit aicpa.org at http://apps.aicpa.org/secure/CPESurvey.aspx.

Course Code: **746460**
CL4FRGNP GS-0416-0A
Revised: **February 2016**

TABLE OF CONTENTS

Chapter 1 1-1

Introduction 1-1

    Overview 1-2

    Introduction 1-3

    General Warning Signs of Fraud 1-4

    Ways to Prevent, Detect, or Deter Fraud 1-6

    Summary 1-9

    Practice Questions 1-10

Chapter 2 2-1

The Governmental and Not-for-Profit Environments 2-1

    Unique Characteristics of the Governmental Environment 2-2

    Governmental Organizations 2-3

    Unique Characteristics of the Not-for-Profit Environment 2-6

    Governmental Financial Reporting Objectives and Users 2-10

    Not-for-Profit Financial Reporting Objectives and Users 2-12

    Summary 2-14

    Practice Questions 2-15

Chapter 3 3-1

The Auditor's Consideration of Fraud in a Financial Statement Audit 3-1

    Auditor Responsibilities and Marketplace Expectations 3-2

    Fraud Risk Factors in Governmental and Not-for-Profit Entities 3-4

Fraud and the Auditor: An Overview 3-9

The Auditor's Responsibilities Related to Fraud 3-11

Application of AU-C Section 240 to Audits of Governmental and Not-for-Profit Entities 3-13

Summary 3-16

Practice Questions 3-17

Chapter 4 4-1

Where Fraud Occurs in Governmental and Not-for-Profit Organizations 4-1

Where Fraud Occurs 4-2

Where Fraud Occurs in Governmental Organizations 4-3

Where Fraud Occurs in Not-for-Profit Entities 4-5

Fraud Risks in Governmental and Not-for-Profit Entities 4-9

Management Override 4-13

Planning Considerations in Audits of Governmental and Not-for-Profit Entities 4-16

Summary 4-17

Practice Questions 4-18

Chapter 5 5-1

Fraud Schemes Found in Governmental and Not-for-Profit Organizations 5-1

Fraudulent Financial Reporting Schemes 5-2

Fraudulent Financial Reporting Revenue Recognition 5-4

Fraudulent Financial Reporting Functional and Fund Classifications 5-12

Misappropriation of Assets Overview 5-15

Misappropriation of Assets Common Fraud Schemes 5-18

Misappropriation of Assets Common Fraud Schemes Procurement and Contracting 5-19

Misappropriation of Assets Common Fraud Schemes Cash Receipts and Fraudulent
Disbursements 5-22

Misappropriation of Assets Common Fraud Schemes Personnel Costs 5-25

Misappropriation of Assets Common Fraud Schemes Property, Plant, and Equipment 5-28

Misappropriation of Assets Common Fraud Schemes Diversion of Program Benefits
and Assets 5-32

Summary 5-35

Practice Questions 5-36

Glossary .... Glossary 1

Index .... Index 1

Solutions .... Solutions 1

Chapter 1 .... Solutions 1

Chapter 2 .... Solutions 2

Chapter 3 .... Solutions 4

Chapter 4 .... Solutions 5

Chapter 5 .... Solutions 7

Users of this course material are encouraged to visit the AICPA website at www.aicpa.org/CPESupplements to access supplemental learning material reflecting recent developments that may be applicable to this course. The AICPA anticipates that supplemental materials will be made available on a quarterly basis.

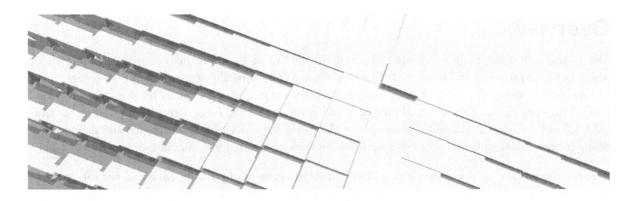

Chapter 1

INTRODUCTION

LEARNING OBJECTIVES

After completing this chapter, you should be able to do the following:

- Determine the general warning signs of fraud.
- Identify characteristics of individuals that perpetrate financial statement fraud.
- Identify general techniques to prevent, detect, or deter fraud.

Overview

This course is designed to give auditors and accounting and finance professionals an understanding of where in the government and not-for-profit environments fraud typically occurs and how to recognize and respond to these risks. With this knowledge, management of governmental or not-for-profit entities is in a better position to develop fraud programs and controls that will be effective in responding to fraud risks. Likewise, such understanding improves the likelihood the auditor of governmental and not-for-profit entities will identify and properly respond to the risk of material misstatement due to fraud.

In short, the purpose of this course is to address how management of governmental and not-for-profit entities and their auditors can recognize and respond to fraud risks that are unique to these entities.

Key Point

Throughout this course, the terms *he* and *she* are used alternately and no discrimination or implications related to either gender is intended. Additionally, this course and its appendixes have been developed using the professional and industry standards, practices, and procedures in effect at the time of the writing. Management, auditors, and other professionals should consult current authoritative guidance in addition to these materials.

Introduction

In the early years of the twenty-first century, the accounting profession experienced some of its darkest days since the 1938 McKesson-Robbins corporate accounting scandal. Massive scandals in the early 2000s at Enron, WorldCom, and Global Crossing put all CPAs in the spotlight whether they were auditors of publicly traded companies or small, closely held family corporations. To protect the American public against such spectacular failures in the future, President George W. Bush signed the Sarbanes-Oxley Act (SOX) into law in the summer of 2002.

It is interesting to note that whereas Statement on Auditing Standards (SAS) No. 99, *Consideration of Fraud in a Financial Statement Audit* (AICPA, *Professional Standards*), which is now clarified and codified as AU-C section 240, *Consideration of Fraud in a Financial Statement Audit* (AICPA, *Professional Standards*), was released after the passage of SOX, it was not issued in response to the failures giving rise to its passage. SAS No. 99 was the result of a four-year process that began with five academic research studies conducted as part of the AICPA Fraud Research Steering Task Force. In addition to these studies, the Public Oversight Board, at the request of the Securities and Exchange Commission, appointed a Panel on Audit Effectiveness in 1998. This Panel conducted its own research primarily related to audit effectiveness and issued a report in August of 2000.

Using these studies and other information, the AICPA Fraud Task Force, established in September of 2000, reviewed the previous guidance in SAS No. 82, *Consideration of Fraud in a Financial Statement Audit*, and concluded it was fundamentally sound. The recommendations of this task force to enhance professional auditing standards related to fraud were incorporated in the exposure draft issued February 28, 2002, which was adopted as SAS No. 99 in October of 2002 and later clarified and codified in AU-C section 240.

Fraud has become a major focus among not only financial statement users but also among many Americans in their roles as investors, watchdogs, philanthropists, or private citizens. In the last several decades, news reports have often revealed fraud and abuse at all levels of governmental and not-for-profit organizations. The national-level United Way scandal of the early 1990s had a significant negative impact on many local United Way agencies. Americans were outraged to learn the federal government had spent thousands of dollars for items that could have been found at the local building supply store for less than $100. Citizens of Dixon, Illinois were shocked to learn of the massive fraud perpetrated by a long-term high-level employee whose family had been a member of the community for generations.

Individuals and businesses contributing to not-for-profit organizations have a legitimate expectation that their donations will be used to further the mission of the not-for-profit organization. When such funds are diverted for other uses, or worse, appropriated for personal gain, the reputation of the not-for-profit organization is jeopardized. In such cases, the lack of trust potential individual and corporate donors have in the not-for-profit organization can seriously affect its revenues and, correspondingly, its continued existence.

For citizens, fraud in governmental organizations is a misuse of the public funds they provided to the government without choice and in good faith. Such breaches of trust further erode their tenuous faith in the "American Way" and needlessly increase the cost of providing public goods and services. Simply put, everyone loses when fraud occurs in governmental organizations.

General Warning Signs of Fraud

Being aware of situations that have the potential to create fraud risks is the first step in designing effective programs and controls to prevent, detect, and deter fraud. The following general situations may be warning signs indicating fraudulent financial reporting or fraud due to misappropriation of assets:

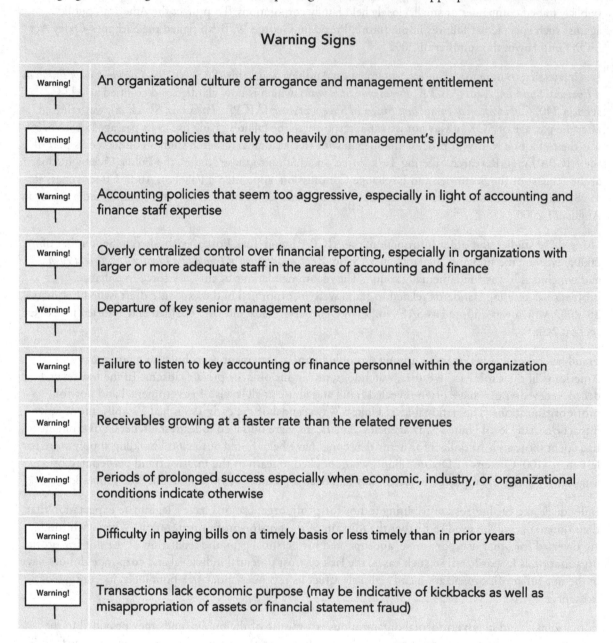

Warning Signs
An organizational culture of arrogance and management entitlement
Accounting policies that rely too heavily on management's judgment
Accounting policies that seem too aggressive, especially in light of accounting and finance staff expertise
Overly centralized control over financial reporting, especially in organizations with larger or more adequate staff in the areas of accounting and finance
Departure of key senior management personnel
Failure to listen to key accounting or finance personnel within the organization
Receivables growing at a faster rate than the related revenues
Periods of prolonged success especially when economic, industry, or organizational conditions indicate otherwise
Difficulty in paying bills on a timely basis or less timely than in prior years
Transactions lack economic purpose (may be indicative of kickbacks as well as misappropriation of assets or financial statement fraud)

KNOWLEDGE CHECK

1. Which is NOT a general warning sign of fraud?

    a. Organizational culture of arrogance and management entitlement.
    b. Overly centralized control over financial reporting.
    c. Open and honest communication between key accounting or finance personnel and top management of the organization.
    d. The entity engages in transactions that lack economic purpose.

Ways to Prevent, Detect, or Deter Fraud

A number of low-cost, high-impact policies and procedures can be implemented to help prevent, detect, and deter fraud in most governmental and not-for-profit organizations. A highly effective and almost no-cost control that can be implemented by any governmental or not-for-profit organization is to *take a hard line* with respect to fraud. If the "tone at the top" is one of zero tolerance and fraudsters are promptly disciplined, employees may be less likely to commit fraud. A *positive and open work environment*, at all levels of the organization, also helps in preventing, detecting, and deterring fraud.

To design effective fraud prevention programs and controls, it is necessary to understand what type of individual typically perpetrates fraud. Fraud research consistently indicates the common characteristics of individuals that perpetrate financial statement fraud are

- a trusted employee,
- dedicated and often works long hours,
- dislikes mandatory vacation policies,
- resents cross-training,
- seen as likeable and generous, and is
- deceptive and usually an adept liar.

GENERAL TECHNIQUES TO PREVENT, DETECT, OR DETER FRAUD

Other general techniques to prevent, detect, or deter fraud include the following:

- *General*
  - Periodic review of control accounts for adjustments when fully integrated subsidiary systems are in place
  - Establishment of a "fraud hotline" (as simple as a board member with a cell phone or as sophisticated as a separate phone line allowing anonymous calls on any day and at any time)

- *Cash*
  - Timely reconciliation of and review of bank statements for
    - unusual activity,
    - dual endorsements on back of checks,
    - changes to items on front of checks, and
    - individuals endorsing checks issued to a business

- *Purchasing/ accounts payable*
  - Extensive paperwork and procedures related to setting up new vendors (especially effective if purchasing is extremely decentralized)
  - When controls and programs related to cash disbursements or purchasing are inadequate, use of a simple software program (internally developed or purchased off the shelf) to
    - cross-reference vendor names to all permutations of employee names;
    - cross-reference vendor payment addresses to all employee addresses;

- cross-reference all delivery locations on vendor statements to all physical addresses of the organization;
- cross-reference phone numbers on vendor statements to employee phone numbers;
- cross-reference all delivery locations on vendor statements to all employee addresses;
- identify vendors with higher than expected purchase volume either for the month or for the year (or some other meaningful period);
- identify transactions (purchases, purchase orders, and checks) falling just below established threshold amounts listed by vendor, purchaser, department/ agency, employee, etc.;
- list vendors with incomplete master file information; and
- list vendors added and deleted within an established time frame.

- *Payroll/ personnel*
  - Mandatory background checks prior to starting work
  - Printing accrued and unused leave hours on employee pay check stubs (deters theft of hours when payroll/ personnel controls are inadequate)
  - Surprise visits to offsite locations

COMPUTER FRAUD

In today's business environment, technology plays a major role in almost all aspects of an organization's operations. The auditor or chief financial officer may be unable to keep up with technological changes. In many of these cases, the establishment of programs and controls to prevent, detect, or deter computer-related fraud is left to the technology function. By understanding the factors that encourage fraud, effective programs and controls that discourage fraud can be developed.

Factors influencing computer crime are either motivational or personal. Motivational and personal factors relate to both rationalization/ attitude and incentive/ pressure in the fraud triangle. The following motivational and personal factors tend to encourage computer fraud:

- Inadequate pay and benefits, including promotional opportunities
- Poor communication of expectations (job performance, behavior, and the like) by management
- Lack of performance feedback mechanisms
- Mediocre performance as an acceptable performance standard
- Inadequate support and lack of resources to meet standards
- Not enough review and follow-up to assure compliance with organizational programs and controls
- Inadequate standards of recruitment and selection
- Deficient or missing orientation and training programs

Preventing computer fraud is not necessarily a highly technical or expensive proposition. The primary factors that discourage computer crime are

- internal accounting controls,
- access controls, and
- Internet firewalls.

Preventing, Detecting, and Deterring Computer Fraud
Separation and rotation of duties both within and external to the technology function
Timely update of accessible computer applications when personnel change jobs or when the requirements of their current position change
Periodic and surprise inspections and security reviews
All control policies and procedures required to be written (zero tolerance for deviations from this policy)
Offline controls and limits such as batch controls and hash totals where indicated and cost-effective

Access controls to prevent, detect, and deter computer fraud include the following:

- Authentication/ identification controls, such as
    - keys,
    - smartcards,
    - passwords,
    - biometrics,
    - callback systems,
    - one-time passwords,
    - constrained access by time and day, and
    - periodic code and password changes

- Compartmentalization of information
- Encryption of data while stored or in transit

KNOWLEDGE CHECK

2. Which is NOT a general technique to prevent, detect, or deter personnel fraud?

    a. Mandatory background checks prior to starting work.
    b. Routine visits to offsite locations.
    c. Printing accrued and unused leave hours on employee pay check stubs.
    d. Performance feedback mechanisms.

Summary

This chapter provided an introduction to fraud including general warning signs of fraud. Additionally, this chapter identified the characteristics of the "typical fraudster" and provided general ways to prevent, detect, and deter fraud. Also discussed in this chapter were general controls that can be implemented to address computer fraud risks.

Practice Questions

1. List three ways to prevent, detect, or deter computer fraud.

2. List three characteristics common to individuals that perpetrate financial statement fraud.

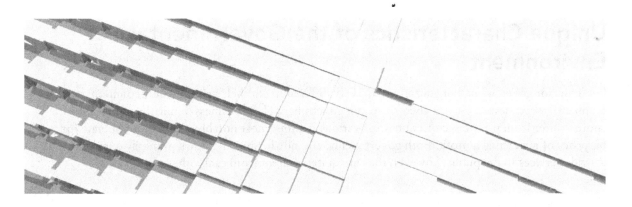

Chapter 2

THE GOVERNMENTAL AND NOT-FOR-PROFIT ENVIRONMENTS

LEARNING OBJECTIVES

After completing this chapter, you should be able to do the following:

- Identify the characteristics and situations that exist in governmental and not-for-profit entities that differentiate them from entities in the private sector.
- Determine how objectives of financial reporting and the users of financial statements of governments and not-for-profit entities differ from those in the private sector.
- Determine how to incorporate the unique financial reporting objectives of governmental and not-for-profit entities in planning and performing audits of these organizations.

Unique Characteristics of the Governmental Environment

Public sector governmental organizations are very different from their private sector counterparts in a number of ways, despite current rhetoric to run government like a business. Similarly, not-for-profit entities differ from private sector entities for various reasons; most notably, they do not operate for purposes of generating a profit. Both governmental and not-for-profit entities primarily operate to provide services to the public; however, they are quite different from each other.

Governmental Organizations

The unique characteristics of governmental organizations are generally as illustrated here.

Unique Characteristics of Governmental Organizations			
Government in the Sunshine	**Public Goods and Services**	**Political Process**	**Lack of a Profit Motive**
They are public organizations.	They provide goods and services to the general public using funds typically secured from involuntary resource providers.	Decisions are made in a political environment.	Goods and services are generally provided without a profit motive.

GOVERNMENT IN THE SUNSHINE

The *primary characteristic* distinguishing governmental organizations from private sector business entities and not-for-profit entities is that they are *public* organizations. Their very nature requires that *business be conducted in view of the public.* It is this very simple aspect on which the financial reporting objectives of governmental financial statements rest. Public governmental organizations differ fundamentally from public business entities[1] that are publicly traded. Even though publicly traded companies are subject to a high level of regulation and public scrutiny, they are not often required to conduct their business in view of the public.

State and local governments are required to operate "in the sunshine" for all meetings in which decisions are to be made that do or may impact the public. This requirement to conduct business in a public forum is often a significant impediment to timely responses to sensitive issues. Though billions of shares of Apple stock are traded annually, the audit committee is allowed to meet behind closed doors. In contrast, the city council of a small rural town in North Florida, serving as an audit committee, must meet in a public forum. Not only is the city council of this small Florida town required to meet in full view of the public but also to adequately and timely publish notice of such meeting and to provide minutes of the meeting to the public.

---

[1] The Financial Accounting Standards Board (FASB) defines a public business entity in Accounting Standards Update (ASU) No. 2013-12, *Definition of a Public Business Entity.*

PUBLIC GOODS AND SERVICES

The *second characteristic* distinguishing governmental organizations from private sector business entities relates to their being public organizations. As such, governmental organizations provide *goods and services that benefit the public at large*. Such public goods and services are provided, in most cases, without regard to how much is paid by those receiving the goods or services. As such, there is no quid pro quo, meaning that nonexchange transactions comprise a significant amount of activity for many governments. Even in cases where the governmental organization intends to recover its costs with user fees, not all costs may be included in determining the fee structure. Often high cost, limited use, and limited or non-revenue producing capital assets (for example police stations, schools, and roads) are needed to provide public goods and services.

To fund the provision of public goods and services, governmental organizations (in most states) are authorized to impose taxes at a number of levels and on a variety of income, goods, or services. This places individuals and businesses in the position of involuntary resource providers.

A variety of legal constraints and controls exist at all levels of government to ensure the resources involuntarily provided by individuals and businesses are expended for the public good. Typically, the budget process in governmental organizations is the most public manifestation of accountability from a fiscal, operational, and planning perspective. Governmental organizations are directly accountable to citizens, taxpayers, and business owners as well as society at large. The annual audit of a governmental organization's financial statements is the most visible evidence of its fiscal accountability.

There is tremendous *pressure on employees of governmental organizations to provide more and better quality public goods and services* using less financial, human, and capital resources. Often, administrative functions such as accounting, internal audit, and procurement *lack sufficient staff to implement or administer an effective system of internal accounting controls*. In addition, many small and medium-sized governmental organizations *lack the financial resources to attract qualified accounting and finance personnel*.

POLITICAL PROCESS

A *third characteristic* that distinguishes governmental organizations from private sector entities and not-for-profit entities is the *political process* since they are public organizations. The political process varies by type, size, and nature of government, but in all cases places constant pressure on elected officials and other policy makers. Elected officials may feel pressure from citizens, special interest groups, other governments, or unfunded governmental mandates. In some cases, elected officials make decisions that are politically correct but not necessarily economically viable or operationally feasible in the short-run or in the future.

Doing More With Less

Elected officials are often hesitant to increase taxes even though citizen demands for public goods and services increase. Such reluctance to adequately fund service needs results in governmental employees being forced to provide more goods and services with fewer financial, human, and capital resources. Over time, this approach can erode the tax base and infrastructure of a governmental organization as well as negatively impact employee morale.

LACK OF A PROFIT MOTIVE

The *final characteristic distinguishing* governmental organizations from private sector entities is the *lack of a profit motive* which is related to the public goods and services they provide and sometimes the political process. Governmental organizations are in the business of providing goods and services that benefit the public or that typically are not provided by private markets but considered to be in the public interest.

Goods and services provided by governmental organizations are often made available to the public at little or no charge, such as recreation services. Other goods and services, such as emergency rescue and transport services, have fee structures with little or no relationship to the benefit received by the consumer or the cost incurred by the governmental organization.

Costs associated with providing some goods and services, such as utilities, are intended to be recovered in full or in part with appropriate user fees. However, there is wide disparity in the costs governmental organizations consider recoverable through utility user fees. For example, some governmental organizations allocate all, or a portion of all, costs of the government to utility operations while others allocate only those costs directly or indirectly associated with utility operations.

KNOWLEDGE CHECK

1. Which is true of governmental organizations?

    a. A unique characteristic of governmental organizations is that they are public organizations.
    b. Governmental organizations do not provide goods or services to the general public using funds secured from involuntary resource providers.
    c. A requirement to conduct business in a public forum is never a significant impediment to timely responses to sensitive issues.
    d. Governments are required to recover all costs through user fees.

Unique Characteristics of the Not-for-Profit Environment

FASB ASC 958-10-20 defines not-for-profit entities for purposes of preparing financial statements in accordance with generally accepted accounting principles.[2] It distinguishes a not-for-profit organization from a business entity based on several characteristics as illustrated in the following table.

Unique Characteristics of Not-for-Profit Entities		
Significant Contributions	**Lack of a Profit Motive**	**Ownership Interests**
Significant amounts of contributions of resources are received from resource providers not expecting commensurate or proportionate financial return.	The organization operates for purposes other than to provide goods or services at a profit.	Ownership interests such as those found in business enterprises are absent.

Entities falling within these guidelines differ from for-profit business entities, not simply from a definitional perspective, but also from their distinctive organizational and operational characteristics.

SIGNIFICANT CONTRIBUTIONS

In order to fund goods or services provided to the community for little or no cost, not-for-profit entities have traditionally relied on contributions from individuals, businesses, and government grants. Contributions and/or grants often represent a significant portion of the total resources available to many not-for-profit entities. Individuals, businesses, and grantors provide funds to a not-for-profit organization with no expectation of financial or other remuneration.

Contributions and grants received by a not-for-profit organization may be *subject to donor/grantor restrictions imposing time or use restrictions* either on a temporary or permanent basis. Such contributions are required to be classified as restricted until the restriction has been lifted or satisfied. Grants are typically restricted for a particular program of the not-for-profit organization. In some cases, grants are used to fully or partially offset the cost of providing goods or services to the community at little or no charge.

Valuable and sometimes *significant services are contributed* on behalf of, or for the benefit of, a not-for-profit organization or the clients it serves. These services may take the form of professional services (such as legal, accounting, auditing, architectural, or engineering) or trade services (such as electrical, plumbing, or maintenance) and would typically be paid for by the not-for-profit organization if not donated by the

---

[2] ASU No. 2013-12 specifically excludes all not-for-profit entities from the definition of a public business entity and from the scope of the *Private Company Decision-Making Framework: A Guide for Evaluating Financial Accounting and Reporting for Private Companies* for the purpose of standard setting.

service providers. Certain types of contributed services are required to be either recognized in the financial statements or disclosed in the notes to the financial statements.

A variety of *legal constraints and controls* exist to ensure the resources provided voluntarily by individuals and businesses are used for the purposes they specified or to further the mission of the not-for-profit organization. *Grant provisions* often require a significant amount of control over and accountability for funds disbursed to not-for-profit entities. In many cases, the *annual audit* of a not-for-profit organization's financial statements is the most visible evidence of its fiscal accountability. Rules and regulations of the Internal Revenue Service related to tax-exempt organizations also act as constraints and controls over contributions received by a not-for-profit organization.

KNOWLEDGE CHECK

2. Which is true of not-for-profit entities?

    a. Contributions received by a not-for-profit organization can never be subject to donor restrictions on the use of those funds.
    b. In order to fund goods or services provided to the community for little or no cost, not-for-profit entities have traditionally relied on contributions from individuals and businesses.
    c. Contributions received by a not-for-profit organization cannot be subject to temporary donor restrictions.
    d. Grant provisions do not typically require that a not-for-profit organization be accountable for the funds disbursed under the provisions of the grant.

LACK OF A PROFIT MOTIVE

Not-for-profit entities are organized for and *operated to achieve a particular mission rather than to make a profit* from their operations. It is this dedication to mission that drives the operations of most not-for-profit entities. To this end, the financial statements of a not-for-profit organization reflect expenses on a functional basis rather than their natural line-item type classifications. (Voluntary health and welfare organizations are required to present both natural and functional expense information.) Additionally, the mission of a not-for-profit organization is what makes it a qualified tax-exempt organization under the Internal Revenue Code.

With a high level of focus on mission, administrative functions such as accounting, internal audit, and procurement are often ignored or seen as unnecessary. Therefore, not-for-profit entities often *lack sufficient staff to implement or administer an effective system of internal accounting controls.* In addition, many small and medium-sized not-for-profit entities *lack the financial resources to attract qualified accounting and finance personnel.*

In furtherance of their missions, not-for-profit entities typically provide goods or services to the community, in many cases, without regard to how much is paid by those receiving the goods or services. Even in cases where the not-for-profit organization intends to recover its costs with fees or charges, not all costs may be included in determining the fee structure. Additionally, there is wide disparity in the costs not-for-profit entities consider recoverable through client charges and fees.

Often not-for-profit entities confuse the *lack of a profit motive* with not being "allowed" to generate a profit. Not-for-profit entities are a business and should therefore consider typical business strategies like adequately covering costs with fees or charges. Simply because they are not profit-motivated does not excuse the not-for-profit organization from acting prudently and exercising sound business judgment. It is not the existence of a positive "bottom line" that differentiates not-for-profit entities from entities in the private sector, but rather the function of the "bottom line." The not-for-profit organization uses excess profits to further its mission while for-profit entities distribute excess profits to owners or for private gain.

OWNERSHIP INTERESTS

Because not-for-profit entities do not have stockholders, the *equity in the not-for-profit entity is represented by its net assets*. Owners of for-profit entities have a viable interest in the equity of the entity in which they are invested. As such, they are able to exercise control over the entity in order to protect their equity interest. There are no "owners" of the typical not-for-profit organization and therefore no "owners" exist to protect the net assets of the not-for-profit organization.

In some states the net assets of a not-for-profit organization are protected through incorporating documents or other legal means. The Internal Revenue Service requires the articles of incorporation for newly recognized tax exempt organizations to include the following language in an effort to protect the net assets of the not-for-profit organization:

> Upon dissolution of the Corporation, assets shall be distributed for one or more exempt purposes within the meaning of section 501(c)(3) of the Internal Revenue Code, or the corresponding section of any future Federal tax code, or shall be distributed to the Federal government, or to a state or local government, for a public purpose. Any such assets not so disposed of shall be disposed of by a Court of Competent Jurisdiction of the county in which the principal office of the Corporation is then located, exclusively for such purposes or to such organization or organizations, as said Court shall determine, which are organized and operated exclusively for such purposes.

OTHER DIFFERENCES

They're Different

Not-for-profit entities differ among themselves even when they may have the same or similar mission. For example, a not-for-profit organization may be a museum in a highly populated metropolitan area or a small church in the rural south, both of which provide different services and serve vastly different populations with diverse needs. Likewise, two not-for-profit hospitals may differ in the services they provide because of their geographic location, the populations they serve, bed capacity, plant and equipment, etc. Management and auditors of not-for-profit entities need to understand not only the differences between not-for-profit entities and private sector entities, but also the differences between various not-for-profit entities.

These differences make it necessary for management and auditors of not-for-profit entities to consider fraud risks differently than fraud risks typically associated with for-profit entities.

KNOWLEDGE CHECK

3. Which is true of not-for-profit entities?

   a. Not-for-profit entities often receive contributions in the form of grants from governmental agencies or other not-for-profit entities.
   b. Contributions received by a not-for-profit organization cannot be subject to permanent donor restrictions.
   c. Not-for-profit entities are organized to make a profit from their operations rather than to achieve a particular mission.
   d. Not-for-profit entities are allowed to have stockholders.

Governmental Financial Reporting Objectives and Users

GOVERNMENTAL FINANCIAL REPORTING OBJECTIVES

Financial reporting objectives of governmental financial statements reflect the needs of the users. The needs of these financial statement users differ in a number of ways from users of private sector financial statements.

Concepts Statement No. 1, *Objectives of Financial Reporting*, of the Governmental Accounting Standards Board (GASB) identifies the objectives of external financial reporting by state and local governments. These objectives include the following:

- To fulfill the government's obligation to be *publicly accountable* and enable users to assess accountability regarding
    - Sufficiency of current revenues to finance current-year services;
    - Compliance with the legally adopted budget and other finance-related legal/ contractual requirements; and
    - Service efforts, costs, and accomplishments of the governmental organization.

Public accountability presumes taxpayers are entitled to know what their governments are doing and how, what they have done and how well, and what they plan to do and why. Citizens as well as legislative and oversight bodies almost universally use financial reporting to assess accountability in their governmental organizations. *Accountability* forces governmental organizations to answer to its citizens and to justify to them the need for public resources as well as the intended and actual use of said public resources.

- To satisfy needs of financial statement users relying on governmental reports as important sources of *information for decision making* related to
    - Evaluating operating results for the fiscal period, and
    - Assessing level of services that can be provided by the government and its ability to meet obligations as they become due.

Decision making encompasses not only economic decisions but social and political decisions as well.

USERS OF GOVERNMENTAL FINANCIAL REPORTS

Governmental financial reports are used internally as well as externally to make decisions or to ensure public accountability. As illustrated in the following table, there are three primary users of external governmental financial reports.

	Three Primary Users of External Governmental Financial Reports
1	*Citizens*—Those to whom governmental organizations are primarily accountable.
2	*Legislative and oversight bodies*—Those directly representing citizens.
3	*Investors and creditors*—Those lending or participating in the lending process, including grantors.

Users of government financial reports assess accountability through traditional measures such as actual to budget comparisons; assessment of financial condition; and compliance with laws, rules, and regulations. Additional non-traditional uses of financial reporting include assisting users in evaluating efficiency and effectiveness.

KNOWLEDGE CHECK

4. Which is true of governmental financial reporting?

    a. Governmental financial reports are used in decision-making and in assessing accountability.
    b. Public accountability ignores that taxpayers are entitled to know what their government is doing and how.
    c. The objectives of external financial reporting by state and local governments do not include the obligation to be publicly accountable.
    d. The primary users of external governmental financial reports include only legislative and oversight bodies.

Not-for-Profit Financial Reporting Objectives and Users

NOT-FOR-PROFIT FINANCIAL REPORTING OBJECTIVES

Financial reporting objectives of not-for-profit financial reports focus on decisions generally made by resource providers primarily because resource providers are important users of financial reports even though they do not have the ability to prescribe information they want to see in financial reports.

Statement of Financial Accounting Concepts No. 4, *Objectives of Financial Reporting by Nonbusiness Organizations*, of the Financial Accounting Standards Board identifies the objectives of external financial reporting by not-for-profit entities. Some of the objectives of financial reporting for not-for-profit entities include

- Broadly focusing on information useful to resource providers and others in making rational resource allocation decisions,
- Narrowing to the information needs of resource providers and others related to services provided by not-for-profit entities and their ability to continue to provide such services, and
- Wrapping up with the types of information financial reporting by not-for-profit entities can provide to meet these needs.

Generally, financial reports provide information *useful in making decisions* regarding the allocation of scarce resources, but they do not determine what those decisions should be. Specific objectives of financial reporting by not-for-profit entities identified in Concepts Statement No. 4 include providing information to present and potential resource providers and other users that is *useful in making rational decisions regarding allocating resources* to not-for-profit entities.

USERS OF FINANCIAL REPORTS OF NOT-FOR-PROFIT ENTITIES

Financial reports of not-for-profit entities are used internally as well as externally to make decisions and to assess information about services provided by the not-for-profit organization. As illustrated in the following table, there are three primary users of external financial reports of not-for-profit entities.

Three Primary Users of External Not-for-Profit Financial Reports

1	*Resource providers*—Includes those that are directly compensated for providing resources (such as lenders, vendors, and employees) and those not directly and proportionately compensated for providing resources (such as members, donors, and taxpayers).
2	*Constituents*—Those who use and benefit from services provided by the not-for-profit organization.
3	*Governing and oversight bodies*—Those responsible for establishing policies and for overseeing and evaluating management of not-for-profit entities (such as boards of directors, trustees, legislatures [federal, state, and local], councils, national headquarters, accrediting agencies, governmental regulatory agencies, and the like).

The various users of financial reports of not-for-profit entities are commonly interested in the following areas:

- Information regarding the services provided by a not-for-profit organization
- How efficient and effective the not-for-profit organization was in providing those services
- The ability of the not-for-profit organization to continue providing those services in the future

In addition to the shared concerns, the individual primary external users of the financial reports of not-for-profit entities have specific areas of interest. Some of the issues specific to particular external users of these financial reports are as follows:

- *Resource providers*, such as donors, may be interested in information indicating how well the not-for-profit organization met its objectives and whether to continue their support of the not-for-profit organization. On the other hand, resource providers such as lenders and vendors are concerned with the ability of the not-for-profit organization to generate cash flow sufficient to pay obligations to them on time.
- *Constituents*, like resource providers, are interested in whether or not the not-for-profit organization is able to continue providing services in the future and, if so, at what cost to constituents.
- *Governing and oversight bodies* use information in financial reports to determine whether management carried out policy mandates with which they were charged. They also use this information to change and/ or develop new policies.

Summary

This chapter provided insight into the unique aspects of governmental and not-for-profit entities that may need to be considered in recognizing and responding to fraud risks. In addition, this chapter focused on how financial reporting objectives and users of governmental and not-for-profit financial statements may impact the recognition of, and response to, fraud risks by management and auditors of not-for-profit entities.

Practice Questions

1. What are the major characteristics differentiating governmental organizations from those in the private sector?

2. What are the major characteristics differentiating not-for-profit entities from those in the private sector?

3. Who are the primary users of external governmental financial reports?

4. Who are the primary users of external not-for-profit financial reports?

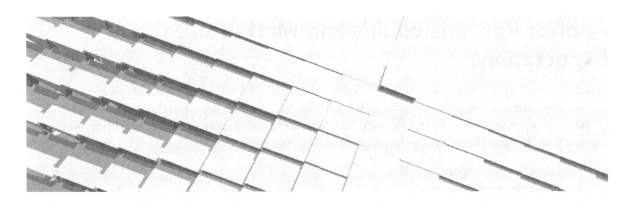

Chapter 3

THE AUDITOR'S CONSIDERATION OF FRAUD IN A FINANCIAL STATEMENT AUDIT

LEARNING OBJECTIVES

After completing this chapter, you should be able to do the following:

- Identify the definition of fraud for financial reporting purposes.
- Identify the fraud risk factors that comprise the fraud triangle.
- Determine the auditor's responsibilities related to fraud under AU-C section 240, *Consideration of Fraud in a Financial Statement Audit* (AICPA, *Professional Standards*).

Auditor Responsibilities and Marketplace Expectations

Fraud is a broad legal concept, and management and those charged with governance of governmental and not-for-profit entities and their stakeholders may confuse the legal aspect of fraud with its definition for financial reporting purposes. In a financial statement audit, the auditor is concerned with fraud that causes a material misstatement in the financial statements as a result of

- fraudulent financial reporting, and
- misappropriation of assets.

AU-C section 240 defines fraud as

> An intentional act by one or more individuals among management, those charged with governance, employees, or third parties, involving the use of deception that results in a misstatement in financial statements that are the subject of an audit.

Key Point

 It may be helpful to discuss the differences between legal and accounting fraud with staff or client personnel. In some cases, staff or clients may approach fraud from its legal rather than accounting definition.

As described in AU-C section 240, the primary responsibility for the prevention and detection of fraud lies with both management and those charged with governance of their respective governmental or not-for-profit organization. However, they may misunderstand fraud in the context of a financial statement audit as well as mistakenly believe the auditor's primary responsibility in an audit is the detection of fraud. Because of this *expectation gap,* governmental and not-for-profit entities may tend to postpone implementation of, or ignore completely, the need for effective internal controls.

Auditors might reasonably presume the expectation gap to occur with their smaller or less sophisticated clients. However, a survey conducted by the AICPA soon after the passage of the Sarbanes-Oxley Act of 2002 indicated the expectation gap also exists with sophisticated business decision makers, investors, and shareholders. Based on over 1,000 interviews with such individuals, *more than 80 percent of this presumably knowledgeable group believed the job of the external auditor was to prevent fraud!*

Guidance established with AU-C section 200, *Overall Objectives of the Independent Auditor and the Conduct of an Audit in Accordance With Generally Accepted Auditing Standards* (AICPA, *Professional Standards*), requires the auditor to obtain *reasonable assurance* as to whether the financial statements as a whole are free from material misstatement, whether due to fraud or error. Reasonable assurance is obtained when the auditor obtains sufficient appropriate evidence to reduce audit risk to an acceptably low level.

It is a high, but not absolute, level of assurance because of the inherent limitations of an audit. For example, it would not likely be cost-effective to look at every transaction recorded for the period under audit. Even if the auditor did look at every transaction, he or she would only see those that are recorded. Therefore, it is not possible – even in this highly unlikely situation – to provide absolute assurance with respect to amounts reported in an entity's financial statements. The potential effects of these inherent limitations are particularly significant in cases of misstatements that result from fraud.

Unfortunately, the concept of *reasonable assurance* is not one that is easily understood by management and those charged with governance or other financial statement users. Governmental and not-for-profit entities have stakeholders that are not present in the private sector such as taxpayers, donors, grantors, and regulators. It is often especially difficult for these groups to grasp the concept of reasonable assurance. When the economy is in decline and citizens are struggling to pay their bills, they are not likely to understand that the auditor did not find or report fraud of any amount.

Key Point

 Due to the nature of evidential matter obtained in an audit engagement, and the characteristics of fraud, it is not possible for the auditor to obtain *absolute assurance* with respect to material misstatements in the financial statements.

KNOWLEDGE CHECK

1. Which is true of AU-C section 240?

    a. AU-C section 240 limits the definition of financial statement fraud to fraudulent financial reporting.
    b. AU-C section 240 limits the definition of financial statement fraud to misappropriation of assets.
    c. AU-C section 240 defines financial statement fraud as fraudulent financial reporting and misappropriation of assets..
    d. AU-C section 240 identifies management as having sole responsibility for the prevention and detection of fraud.

Fraud Risk Factors in Governmental and Not-for-Profit Entities

AU-C section 240 defines fraud risk factors as events or conditions that

- indicate an *incentive or pressure* to perpetrate fraud,
- provide an *opportunity* to commit fraud, and
- indicate *rationalizations* to justify a fraudulent action.

These fraud risk factors are most often referred to as the "fraud triangle."

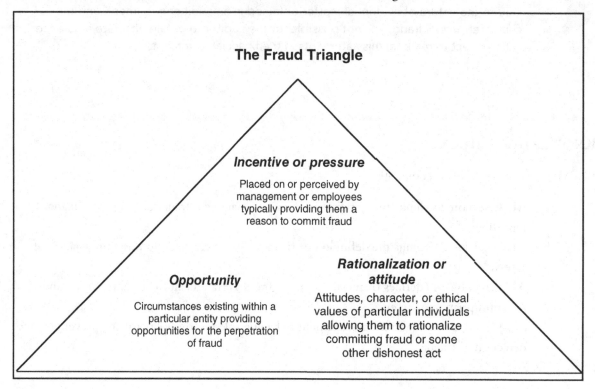

The Fraud Triangle

Incentive or pressure

Placed on or perceived by management or employees typically providing them a reason to commit fraud

Opportunity

Circumstances existing within a particular entity providing opportunities for the perpetration of fraud

Rationalization or attitude

Attitudes, character, or ethical values of particular individuals allowing them to rationalize committing fraud or some other dishonest act

The existence of all three of these conditions may indicate the risk of material misstatement due to fraud exists. However, it is not necessary that any or all of these conditions be present for the auditor to conclude that identified fraud risks exist. Fraud risks may be identified using other criteria or characteristics, such as

- entity size,
- complexity of the entity, or
- ownership attributes of the entity.

GOVERNMENTAL AND NOT-FOR-PROFIT ENTITIES AND THE FRAUD TRIANGLE

Incentive or Pressure

When the economy is in decline, there is often added pressure on governmental and not-for-profit entities to provide services. Governmental organizations feel *pressure* to provide more and higher quality services at a time when elected officials are reluctant to increase tax rates or user charges. In addition, governmental organizations are under pressure to not exceed budgeted expenditure targets or to meet budgeted revenues.

Management of not-for-profit entities may feel pressure to meet or exceed service level targets for both outputs and outcomes. As such, there may be an *incentive* to overstate revenues or to apply revenue recognition criteria that is not in accordance with generally accepted accounting principles. Even when the economy is not in a state of decline, not-for-profit entities may have an *incentive* to overstate revenues or results in an effort to obtain additional grant funds or contributions from resource providers.

Opportunity

The lack of personnel or the lack of sufficiently qualified personnel is prevalent in administrative and accounting and finance functions in both government and not-for-profit entities. The resulting lack of, or ineffective, internal controls creates *opportunities* for fraud. In addition, employees of governmental and not-for-profit entities may work all hours and days of the week. Internal controls may be missing or do not adequately address these situations which may create opportunities for employees working these hours to commit fraud.

Governmental and not-for-profit entities may have a number of locations taking cash in payment of services. In the case of the not-for-profit organization, significant amounts of cash may be received at either central or offsite locations. Additionally, such cash may be collected by persons, such as volunteers, lacking knowledge of existing internal controls. Lacking or ineffective controls in either type of organization create *opportunities* for fraud in these areas.

In the case of the governmental organization, it is highly likely the amounts of many of the revenues received in cash or received at offsite locations are not material to the financial statements taken as a whole. However, one of the objectives of financial reporting for governmental organizations is public accountability. Therefore, situations such as these, while not material to the financial statements, are material to public accountability.

Rationalization or Attitude

Employees of governmental and not-for-profit entities are often paid less than their counterparts in the private sector. Some employees of governmental and not-for-profit entities often rationalize the misappropriation of physical assets as compensation for their low salary levels. Again such situations may not result in material misstatements of financial amounts. They are, however, violations of the public trust and serve as a measure of accountability. Governmental organizations typically keep the permanent employee population at the lowest level possible in an effort toward public accountability. As such, employees of governmental organizations are often over-worked or asked to work out of class without additional compensation. It is common for governmental organizations to not allow two employees to simultaneously fill the same budgeted position. This makes it next to impossible for the incumbent to train their replacement. These specific situations may create an attitude within governmental employees that may then provide them with the *rationale* needed to perpetuate fraud.

Employees of not-for-profit entities may feel pressured to appear efficient and effective in order to attract donors and or to obtain grant funds. These circumstances, added to the pressure to continue to provide a high level of service, may create an environment in which employees are able to *rationalize* perpetrating fraud.

Employees in governmental and not-for-profit entities may also rationalize dishonest acts because they are often paid less than individuals in the private sector. In addition, employees of governmental and not-for-profit entities may work long hours for these lower wages (or perceived to be lower by the employee) or days outside the traditional work week.

A number of governmental and not-for-profit entities are relatively small in either or both dollar volume or number of employees. This and the lack of ownership attributes in governmental and not-for-profit entities may indicate fraud risks for the auditor to consider in planning and conducting the audit engagement. Research based on actual frauds indicates that the existence of "owners" is sometimes a fraud deterrent as employees are less prone to defraud an actual person – especially when they know the owners may have worked long and hard to make their company a success.

PROFESSIONAL SKEPTICISM

Auditors are required by AU-C section 200 to maintain professional skepticism throughout an audit in order to *recognize the possibility* that a material misstatement due to fraud could exist. The potential that a material misstatement may occur due to fraud is considered exclusive of the auditor's past experience with the honesty and integrity of entity management and those charged with governance. When a long-term relationship exists between the auditor and management and those charged with governance, this may be more difficult especially when no fraud or other irregularities have been noted at any time during the auditor-client relationship.

As characterized in AU-C section 200, professional skepticism is an *attitude* that requires the auditor to

- have a questioning mind *and*
- critically assess audit evidence.

This attitude of professional skepticism is to be present throughout and during all aspects of the audit engagement and exercised at all times by the entire engagement team. This may prove challenging for those auditors who have been assigned to a particular audit engagement for a number of years with various levels of responsibilities over that time.

Based on psychology and social science research, the six characteristics of professional skepticism are

- having a questioning mind, including the disposition to view responses and other evidence with some sense of doubt;
- suspension of judgment until appropriate evidence is obtained;
- searching for knowledge and investigating beyond the obvious in obtaining corroborating evidence;
- autonomy by possessing self-direction and moral independence, as well as a conviction to decide for oneself;
- self-esteem or the self-confidence to resist persuasion and to challenge assumptions.

Less experienced members of the audit engagement team may better understand their professional responsibilities with respect to professional skepticism in light of these characteristics. In addition, it may be helpful if these characteristics are discussed during the planning of the audit by all members of the engagement team.

KNOWLEDGE CHECK

2. Which is true of AU-C section 200?

    a. AU-C section 200 requires the auditor to exercise professional skepticism in all audits.

    b. AU-C section 200 requires the auditor to exercise professional skepticism only when considering fraud.

    c. AU-C section 200 requires the auditor to exercise professional skepticism only in first year audits.

    d. AU-C section 200 requires only less experienced members of the audit engagement team to exercise professional skepticism.

Professional Skepticism and Fraud in the Workplace[1]

Research indicates the potential for material fraud exists in the American workplace; therefore, auditors need to be aware of where such fraud could occur. According to a survey sponsored by Ernst & Young LLP, 20 percent of American workers are personally aware of fraud in the workplace. Respondents to this survey estimated employers lost 20 percent of every dollar to some type of workplace fraud and were personally aware of fraud due to the following:

- Theft of office items
- Claiming extra hours worked
- Expense accounts
- Taking kickbacks from suppliers

Some governmental organizations are required by state statute, local ordinance, or policy to periodically rotate auditors. However, for many governmental organizations, no such mandatory rotation of auditors is required. Some not-for-profit entities may be required by their own policies or bylaws to periodically rotate auditors. In some cases, not-for-profit entities representing independent local affiliates of a national organization may be required by the national organization to rotate auditors. However, for many not-for-profit entities, no such mandatory rotation of auditors is required.

As illustrated in the following chart, often *long-term and close relationships* develop between the auditor and governmental or not-for-profit entity. Such relationships may affect the engagement team's ability to truly exercise professional skepticism when there is a long-term relationship between the audited entity and the auditor.

---

[1] "Fraud: The Unmanaged Risk, 8th Global Survey" ©2003. Ernst & Young. All rights reserved.

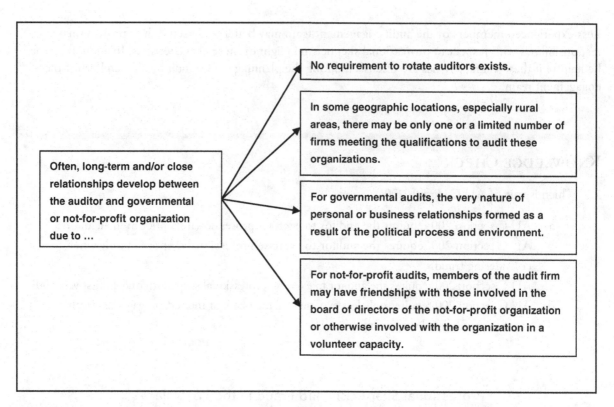

Often, long-term and/or close relationships develop between the auditor and governmental or not-for-profit organization due to …

- No requirement to rotate auditors exists.

- In some geographic locations, especially rural areas, there may be only one or a limited number of firms meeting the qualifications to audit these organizations.

- For governmental audits, the very nature of personal or business relationships formed as a result of the political process and environment.

- For not-for-profit audits, members of the audit firm may have friendships with those involved in the board of directors of the not-for-profit organization or otherwise involved with the organization in a volunteer capacity.

For those auditors with long-term or close relationships with their governmental and not-for-profit clients, it may be challenging to adopt the required level of professional skepticism. Even when auditors feel they have assumed the level of professional skepticism professional standards require, the "appearance" of professional skepticism may not be apparent to those outside the audit firm.

Some audit firms have a limited number of professionals with the requisite training and experience to work on audits of governmental and not-for-profit entities. This may result in assigning the same individuals to the audit of a particular governmental or not-for-profit entity for a number of years in a variety of engagement capacities.

Long-term auditor-client relationships and multiyear assignment of professional staff to a particular audit engagement may give the auditor a false sense of security with respect to the organization under audit. In these situations (whether or not a long-term relationship exists between the auditor and the organization), engagement and firm staff may believe client personnel to be honest and to act with integrity. Because it may be difficult for members of the engagement team to exercise appropriate professional skepticism in these circumstances, they may need to make a conscious effort to put aside past relationships and experiences with the audited entity.

Fraud and the Auditor: An Overview

The auditor's responsibility to form an opinion as to whether an entity's financial statements are free of material misstatement due to error or fraud existed long before the issuance of Statement on Auditing Standards (SAS) No. 99, *Consideration of Fraud in a Financial Statement Audit*, in 2002 (now clarified and codified as AU-C section 240. The objectives of the auditor with respect to AU-C section 240 are to

- identify and assess the risks of material misstatement of the financial statements due to fraud;
- obtain sufficient appropriate audit evidence regarding the assessed risks of material misstatement due to fraud, through designing and implementing appropriate responses; and
- respond appropriately to fraud or suspected fraud identified during the audit.

As such, AU-C section 240 expands the auditor's responsibilities relating to

- understanding the audited entity and its environment,[2]
- responding to assessed risks of material misstatement,[3] and
- evaluating audit evidence.[2]

A Word About Collusion

If *collusion* among management, employees, and third parties exists, even an auditor that performs an audit in accordance with all relevant standards may erroneously conclude the financial statements are free of material misstatements due to fraud.

KNOWLEDGE CHECK

3. Which is an objective of AU-C section 240?

    a. Identify and assess the risks of all misstatement due to fraud.
    b. Notify local law enforcement when fraud is identified.
    c. Obtain sufficient appropriate audit evidence regarding the assessed risks of material misstatement due to fraud.
    d. Respond only to known fraud identified during the audit.

MISSTATEMENTS DUE TO FRAUD

Misstatements relevant to the auditor's consideration of fraud arise from

- *fraudulent financial reporting*, which is the intentional misstatements or omissions (amounts or disclosures) designed to deceive financial statement users, and

---

[2] See AU-C section 315, *Understanding the Entity and Its Environment and Assessing the Risks of Material Misstatement* (AICPA *Professional Standards*) for the full text of these responsibilities.

[3] See AU-C section 330, *Performing Audit Procedures in Response to Assessed Risks and Evaluating the Audit Evidence Obtained*, (AICPA *Professional Standards*) for the full text of these responsibilities.

- *misappropriation of assets,* meaning the theft of an entity's assets or causing an entity to pay for goods or services it did not receive.

FRAUDULENT FINANCIAL REPORTING

Fraudulent financial reporting does not necessarily result from a grandiose plan to deceive financial statement users. Management may simply rationalize material misstatements as an aggressive interpretation of complex accounting issues or as temporary misstatements expected to be corrected when operations subsequently improve. Such fraudulent financial reporting often results from *management override* of existing controls and it may be difficult to detect because management

- withholds evidence,
- misrepresents information in response to auditor inquiries, or
- falsifies documents.

Other more elaborate fraudulent financial reporting schemes may be accomplished through any or all of the following:

- *Manipulation, falsification, or alteration* of accounting records or supporting documentation

- *Misrepresentations or intentional omissions* related to
    - events,
    - transactions, or
    - other significant information.

- *Intentional misapplication of accounting principles* relating to
    - amounts,
    - classification,
    - manner of presentation, or
    - disclosure.

MISAPPROPRIATION OF ASSETS

AU-C section 240 addresses misappropriation of assets only to the extent the effects of such misappropriations cause a *material misstatement* in the financial statements. Most often the misappropriation of assets is accompanied by false or misleading records or other supporting documents. Such false or misleading documentation is possible because internal controls are either missing or circumvented. Typically these types of misappropriations occur through

- embezzlement of receipts,
- stealing assets, and
- causing the entity to pay for goods or services it has not received.

The Auditor's Responsibilities Related to Fraud

OVERVIEW OF THE AUDITOR'S CONSIDERATION OF FRAUD IN A FINANCIAL STATEMENT AUDIT[4]

Management and those charged with governance of governmental and not-for-profit entities are primarily responsible for the prevention and detection of fraud. The responsibilities of the auditor with respect to the consideration of fraud in a financial statement audit in AU-C section 240 include the following:

- Maintaining *professional skepticism* throughout the audit

- *Brainstorming* among members of the engagement team about
    - how and where the audited entity's financial statements might be susceptible to material misstatement due to fraud;
    - how management could perpetrate and conceal fraudulent financial reporting; and,
    - how assets of the entity could be misappropriated

- Performing *risk assessment procedures and related activities* as required by AU-C section 315, *Understanding the Entity and Its Environment and Assessing the risks of Material Misstatement* (AICPA *Professional Standards*), to obtain information for use in identifying the risks of material misstatement due to fraud. Specific requirements include the following:
    - Discussions with management and others within the entity
    - Obtaining an understanding of how those charged with governance exercise oversight of management's processes for identifying and responding to the risks of fraud and the internal control management has established to mitigate these risks
    - Inquiring of those charged with governance to determine their views about the risks of fraud and whether they have knowledge of any actual, suspected, or alleged fraud affecting the entity
    - Evaluating whether identified unusual or unexpected relationships indicate risk of material misstatement due to fraud
    - Considering whether any other information obtained indicates risks of material misstatement due to fraud
    - Evaluating fraud risk factors

- *Identifying and assessing the risks of material misstatement* due to fraud

- *Responding to the assessed risks* of material misstatement due to fraud including the following:
    - Overall responses such as the following:

        - Assignment of staff
        - Evaluation of whether selection and application of accounting policies by management indicates fraudulent financial reporting through earnings management or a bias creating a material misstatement

---

[4] A detailed discussion of the auditor's responsibilities under AU-C section 240 is beyond the scope of this chapter and this course.

- Incorporation of an element of unpredictability in the selection of the nature, timing, and extent of audit procedures
  - Audit procedures responsive to

    - Assessed risks of material misstatement due to fraud at the assertion level;
    - Risks related to management override of controls; and,
    - Other audit procedures to respond to identified risks of management override of controls

- *Evaluating the audit evidence* obtained to determine, among other things, whether the financial statements are materially misstated as a result of fraud

- *Communicating* identified or suspected fraud to
  - Management and those charged with governance (as appropriate), and
  - Regulatory and enforcement authorities if required

- *Documenting*, at a minimum, the following:
  - Significant decisions reached by the engagement team during the brainstorming session regarding

    - Susceptibility of the entity's financial statements to material misstatement due to fraud, and
    - How and when the discussion occurred, and
    - Engagement team members participating in the session
  - Responses to the assessed risks of material misstatement:

    - Due to fraud at the financial statement level
    - Nature, timing and extent of audit procedures performed in response to the assessed risks
    - Linkage of the procedures performed with the assessed risks of material misstatement due to fraud at the assertion level
    - Results of audit procedures designed to address the risk of management override of controls
  - Communications about fraud made to management and those charged with governance
  - If applicable, the auditor's reasons for concluding that there is not a risk of material misstatement due to fraud related to revenue recognitions

KNOWLEDGE CHECK

4. Which is NOT a specific risk assessment procedure required under AU-C section 240?

    a. Obtain an understanding of how those charged with governance exercise oversight of management's processes for identifying and responding to fraud risks.
    b. Discuss fraud risks with management and others within the entity.
    c. Ask employees how assets of the entity could be misappropriated.
    d. Evaluate whether identified unusual or unexpected relationships indicate risk of material misstatement.

Application of AU-C Section 240 to Audits of Governmental and Not-for-Profit Entities

Several areas may be challenging for the auditor to apply the requirements of AU-C section 240 in the audit of a governmental or not-for-profit entity.

ANALYTICAL PROCEDURES PERFORMED AS PART OF RISK ASSESSMENT PROCEDURES

Many governments and not-for-profit entities are interested in the day-to-day cash position of the organization and therefore may only record various accrual-based transactions at the end of the fiscal period. For example, not-for-profit entities may not record transactions in the proper net asset class except at year-end. In small and medium-size governmental and not-for-profit entities, staff may not possess the requisite expertise, or have the time, to record all amounts required under *generally accepted accounting principles* (GAAP) on an interim basis – or even at the end of the fiscal period.

Governmental organizations are highly unlikely to prepare, or regularly prepare, government-wide financial statements on an interim basis. Instead, a government may focus more on budgetary accounting and reporting throughout the fiscal period rather than that which is required under GAAP. In some cases, there may be significant differences between information prepared on the government's budget basis compared to that required under GAAP.

For analytical procedures performed as part of the auditor's risk assessment process, these situations might create "unexpected" relationships for the auditor. For example, interim information might be grossly incomplete such that it makes preliminary analytical procedures highly ineffective. In some situations, the interim information from one year to the next may reflect different levels of "completeness" or conformity with GAAP. Both of these situations may exist in many audits of governmental and not-for-profit entities where staff does not have the expertise or time to produce interim information that is in accordance with GAAP.

While the situations discussed above are not all-inclusive, they will likely affect the auditor's risk of material misstatement due to fraud. Therefore, the auditor may need to ask the governmental or not-for-profit entity to provide information to convert the interim information to a basis consistent with that of the prior audit period or GAAP (or both).

INQUIRIES OF MANAGEMENT AND THOSE CHARGED WITH GOVERNANCE

In small and medium-size governmental or not-for-profit entities, there may be few, if any, management employees with sufficient knowledge to respond to many or some of the auditor's inquiries. The auditor may find it necessary to identify who should respond and then educate them regarding certain aspects of fraud. This may be extremely challenging for the auditor, depending on how wide the *expectation gap* might be.

Public safety functions in governmental organizations are typically *hierarchical in nature* and in some governmental organizations this hierarchical attitude may also represent the tone at the top of the organization. In such cases, the auditor may find it difficult to obtain open and honest responses from employees that are low in the hierarchy of the department, division, or organization. Inquiries made of management or those charged with governance of the governmental organization may adopt an arrogant attitude with engagement team members. Additionally, management and those charged with governance of this type of an organization may be less than forthcoming with answers and explanations for the audit engagement team.

Evaluation of Fraud Prevention Programs and Controls

Governmental and not-for-profit entities may not have staff with the requisite expertise to design effective fraud prevention, detection, and deterrence programs. Additionally, there may be too few administrative or accounting and finance personnel to design, implement, administer, and monitor such programs and controls. This may be especially true in smaller governmental or not-for-profit entities. When such circumstances exist, the auditor may need to consider how they would or would not affect their overall or specific responses to the risk of material misstatement due to fraud.

In some governmental or not-for-profit entities there may be little turnover in accounting, technology, or other support staff. As a result, personnel who originally designed either all or portions of the internal control system may be asked to evaluate their effectiveness in preventing, deterring, and detecting fraud. Therefore, it is important for the auditor to ascertain who designed the controls and programs of interest and who is responsible for maintaining these systems. In these cases, the auditor should exercise a high degree of professional skepticism, as control system designers might not provide a totally objective evaluation of their programs and controls.

Consideration of Management Override of Internal Control

Regardless of the type or size of the audited entity, AU-C section 240 requires the auditor to consider management override as a fraud risk. Specific procedures should be performed with respect to the following:

- Examining *journal entries* and other adjustments
- Performing retrospective reviews of *accounting estimates* for biases
- Understanding the business rationale for significant *unusual transactions*

Journal Entries and Estimates

In small and medium-size governmental or not-for-profit entities, there may be few, if any, employees with sufficient knowledge to prepare journal entries or to develop various accounting estimates. The auditor may conclude in these cases that there is little or no risk of *management override* in these areas due to the apparent lack of technical expertise. However, the auditor may want to consider that there could be a risk of fraudulent financial reporting due to management override in the origination and coding of transactions rather than due to the journal entry or estimation process.

Larger governmental or not-for-profit entities may have only one knowledgeable person who is responsible for developing estimates, preparing and entering journal entries, and preparing the financial statements. In these cases there may be few, if any, controls over these functions which, when coupled with *pressure or rationalization*, could create *opportunity* for that individual to intentionally misstate information in the financial statements.

In some governmental or not-for-profit entities internal control, in the form of a higher level of approval, may exist over *estimates and journal entries*. However, individuals approving estimates may not have the requisite expertise to understand how an estimate was developed or whether the sources of data supporting the estimate are reasonable and reliable. Likewise, individuals approving journal entries may lack the detailed accounting knowledge to know whether the journal entry and the accounts it affects are reasonable and appropriate. In addition, when those approving journal entries question the purpose of and accounts involved in an entry they most likely direct those questions to the individual preparing the journal entry!

Significant Unusual Transactions

While governments are required to conduct all, or almost all, of the business of the government in full view of the public, it does not necessarily follow that such business decisions will be based in rationale thought. In some cases, the political aspects of an issue may far outweigh the underlying business rationale of the transaction. Those charged with governance of both governmental and not-for-profit entities may be more apt to make a decision based on service demands rather than the economics supporting, or not, entering into the transaction. This may be problematic for the auditor of governmental or not-for-profit entities when evaluating the rationale for significant unusual transactions.

REQUIRED AUDITOR COMMUNICATIONS

Many governmental and not-for-profit entities receive significant amounts of *governmental financial assistance*. Therefore, auditors of these organizations may wish to determine during the planning phase of the engagement whether there is a potential need to communicate to funding agencies regarding any evidence of actual or potential fraud. It may also be necessary for the auditor to remind management and those charged with governance of governmental or not-for-profit entities receiving federal or state financial assistance of these communication responsibilities.

AU-C section 240 requires the auditor to communicate certain matters on a timely basis to management and those charged with governance when the auditor has identified a fraud or has obtained information that indicates a fraud may exist. Those charged with governance may want to only be informed when the auditor has identified actual fraud. Communication of suspected fraud is often difficult for those charged with governance to take seriously since they don't see it as an actual issue to address.

In addition, communication of fraud-related matters to management and those charged with governance may be especially difficult in not-for-profit entities due to

- general feeling that all people are "good" and not capable of intentionally causing harm to others (this may be especially challenging when communicating to faith-based not-for-profit entities);
- fear of alienating current and future donors;
- belief that others will see the organization as being easily duped;
- suspected employees may be long-term employees;
- management feels "guilty" for allowing an environment conducive to fraud;
- amounts are considered small or the perpetrator was "justified" in misappropriating organizational assets.

Summary

This chapter focused on the auditor's responsibilities with respect to the consideration of fraud in a financial statement audit and how those responsibilities may be carried out in audits of governmental or not-for-profit entities. The chapter also discussed fraud risks in general and in the specific context of the audit of a governmental or not-for-profit entity. Additionally, this chapter discussed the auditor's requirement to exercise professional skepticism throughout the audit as well as the characteristics of professional skepticism.

Practice Questions

1. In addition to the three fraud conditions identified in AU-C section 240, what two additional areas are identified as potential fraud risks the auditor is required to consider in assessing total fraud risk?

2. How might a close or long-term relationship between a governmental or not-for-profit entity and its auditor affect the auditor's professional skepticism?

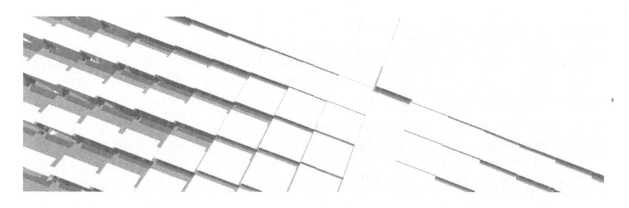

Chapter 4

WHERE FRAUD OCCURS IN GOVERNMENTAL AND NOT-FOR-PROFIT ORGANIZATIONS

LEARNING OBJECTIVES

After completing this chapter, you should be able to do the following:

- Identify the steps of the typical fraud process.
- Analyze the areas where fraud may occur in governmental and not-for-profit entities.
- Identify where fraud risks may exist in governmental and not-for-profit entities.
- Determine where fraud risks may be present related to revenue recognition and management override.

Where Fraud Occurs

With respect to how and where fraud occurs, governmental and not-for-profit entities share a number of areas in common with private sector entities. Fraud in the private sector as well as in governmental and not-for-profit entities occurs in

- overstatement of earnings or increases in net assets,
- fictitious revenues,
- improper revenue recognition,
- understatement of expenses or expenditures,
- overstatement of assets,
- understatement of allowances for receivables,
- overstatement of inventories due to inclusion of obsolete goods, and
- overstatement of property values and creation of fictitious assets.

> The process of fraud is typically the same for all types of entities and occurs in the following three-step process:
>
> - The fraud is committed.
> - Perpetrators receive the benefits of the fraud.
> - The fraud is concealed.

Fraud is typically detected after it is concealed; and the concealment, or lack of concealment, of fraudulent transactions most often is reflected by

- *discrepancies in the accounting records*—Lack of supporting documentation;
- *conflicting or missing evidential matter*—Missing documentation or inconsistent documentation; and
- *problematic or unusual relationships between the auditor and the client*—Unusual delays in providing requested information.

Management and auditors do not usually observe fraud as it is committed. In addition, they may not recognize when the perpetrator of the fraud realizes the benefits of their fraudulent behavior. In most cases, fraud is detected when, or after, the perpetrator attempts to conceal the fraudulent act. Therefore, fraud programs and controls as well as audit procedures need to consider this in order to be effective.

Where Fraud Occurs in Governmental Organizations

There are a number of areas of concern that are unique to governmental organizations with respect to the potential for fraud. Some of these unique areas are illustrated in the following sections.

FUND ACCOUNTING

Using the fund structure, governmental organizations may be able to conceal, misrepresent, or manipulate transactions whether with the intent to defraud or not. Many governmental officials and employees may find it easy to rationalize improper fund transactions or accounting for a number of reasons including the following:

- Maintains current tax levels
- Maintains current user fee levels
- The belief that no one understands fund accounting
- The belief that all financial resources should be available for all operations of the governmental organization regardless of external restrictions

INTERFUND ACTIVITY

Interfund transactions may be used to conceal a number of irregularities which may result in fraudulent financial reporting if not detected. Examples of potentially fraudulent transactions and activities include offsetting operating losses in business-type activities, concealing budget shortfalls, infusing working capital to meet bond covenant ratios, and a number of other transactions. Provisions of Governmental Accounting Standards Board (GASB) Statement No. 34, *Basic Financial Statements—and Management's Discussion and Analysis—for State and Local Governments*, as amended, require disclosure of interfund activity balances by purpose.

FUNCTIONAL ALLOCATION OF EXPENSES

GASB Statement No. 34, as amended, requires the reporting of expenses at the government-wide level by functional classification in the statement of activities. In the statement of activities, functional expenses are offset by specifically identifiable grants (operating and capital) and charges for services. Some governmental agencies may misstate functional amounts to circumvent legal requirements or to comply with grant provisions or bond covenants.

Some states restrict the amount of building permit revenues to the costs of providing protective inspection services and the related administrative costs. In these states, excess building permit revenues must be returned to the community or the permit holder(s). This might be a concern for a particular local governmental organization if they are experiencing a sustained high level of growth or operate very efficiently. In these cases, it is possible building permit fees could exceed the cost of providing protective inspection services.

INTERNAL ACCOUNTING CONTROLS

As in audits of for-profit entities, internal accounting controls are also of concern in audits of governmental organizations. The internal control structure of many governmental organizations lacks the staff or lacks qualified staff in administrative or accounting and finance functions. This results usually in improper segregation of duties, a high level of error in recording transactions, and missing or ineffective control systems.

Another unique aspect of governmental organizations with respect to the consideration of fraud is that of employee compensation and longevity. Typically, many employee classes in the public sector are paid less than their counterparts in the private sector. Ironically, public sector employees tend to have greater time in position and increased overall longevity. These factors considered with limited administrative or accounting and finance functions represent textbook conditions for fraud.

REPEAT SIGNIFICANT DEFICIENCIES, MATERIAL WEAKNESSES, AND OTHER MATTERS RELATED TO INTERNAL CONTROL

Many of the internal control weaknesses discussed previously often result in significant deficiencies or material weaknesses. In some governmental organizations there may be a strong mindset toward providing services to stakeholders at the expense of administrative support functions. As a result, deficiencies in internal control may continue to exist for a number of years. This may also hold true for other matters related to internal control repeated from year to year.

From an audit planning perspective, the auditor of a governmental organization may need to consider these situations as fraud risk factors. The reasons for not implementing other matters related to internal control recommendations or not correcting significant deficiencies may indicate an attitude of rationalization throughout the entire governmental organization. Additionally, the continued existence of missing or ineffective internal controls might create incentives and opportunities for fraud to occur.

KNOWLEDGE CHECK

1. Which is NOT true related to governmental organizations and the allocation of functional expenses?

    a. Governmental organizations would never intentionally misstate functional expenses.

    b. Governmental organizations may intentionally misstate functional expenses to circumvent legal requirements.

    c. Governmental organizations may intentionally misstate functional expenses to comply with bond covenants.

    d. GASB Statement No. 34, as amended, requires the reporting of expenses at the government-wide level by functional classification in the statement of activities.

Where Fraud Occurs in Not-for-Profit Entities

There are a number of areas of concern that are unique to not-for-profit entities with respect to the potential for fraud. Some of these unique areas are illustrated in this chart.

Contributions received from resource providers	Goods or services not provided at a profit	Lack of ownership interests	Related-party transactions
Other areas	Unique Areas of Concern in Not-for-Profit Engagements		Functional allocation of expenses
Split-interest agreements	Repeat significant deficiencies, material weaknesses, and other matters related to internal control		Internal accounting controls

SIGNIFICANT CONTRIBUTIONS

Not-for-profit entities often rely on contributions from individuals and businesses to fund the services they provide as part of their mission. Such contributions are often significant to the total resources available to the entity.

In addition, contributions or grant monies received by an entity may be *subject to donor or grantor restrictions imposing time or use restrictions* either on a temporary or permanent basis. Such contributions are required to be classified as restricted until the restriction has been lifted or satisfied. Management of an entity might be tempted to classify such contributions as unrestricted resources to provide more flexibility in fulfilling the mission of the organization.

Valuable and sometimes *significant services are contributed* on behalf of, or for the benefit of, the entity or the clients it serves. Depending on the type of contributed services, they are required to be either recorded in the financial statements or disclosed in the notes to the financial statements. Because these transactions are required to be reported at fair value, the potential exists for management to aggressively estimate these amounts.

LACK OF A PROFIT MOTIVE

Not-for-profit entities are organized for and *operated to achieve a particular mission rather than to make a profit* from their operations. It is this dedication to mission that drives the operations of not-for-profit entities. In furtherance of their missions, not-for-profit entities may provide goods or services to the community without regard to how much is paid by those receiving the goods or services. Even in cases where the not-for-profit organization intends to recover its costs with fees or charges, not all costs may be included in determining the fee structure.

OWNERSHIP INTERESTS

Not-for-profit entities do not have stockholders; therefore, the *equity in the entity is represented by its net assets*. Because there are no "owners" in an entity, no "owners" exist to protect the net assets of the entity.

KNOWLEDGE CHECK

2. Which is an area unique to not-for-profit entities that may be a target for the potential for fraud?

    a. Contributions.
    b. Payroll.
    c. Owner profitability.
    d. Revenue recognition.

RELATED-PARTY TRANSACTIONS

In a number of not-for-profit entities, individuals are selected to serve on the board of directors based on the financial or economic resources available to them in other capacities. At times, management of the not-for-profit entity may draw on these connections in securing financial, human, or capital resources. These types of transactions may represent below-market transactions or may not be arm's-length in nature. In any event, such transactions may require disclosure in the financial statements as related-party transactions.

Local independent not-for-profit entities may be affiliated with regional, national, or international not-for-profit entities. Transactions with and among these entities may require disclosure in the financial statements as related-party transactions as well.

FUNCTIONAL ALLOCATION OF EXPENSES

Financial Accounting Standards Board (FASB) Accounting Standards Codification™ (ASC) Topic 958 requires not-for-profit voluntary health and welfare entities to report expenses by functional and natural classifications in a matrix format. Other not-for-profit entities are required by FASB ASC 958 to report expenses by functional classification and are encouraged to provide information about their natural expense classification. Some not-for-profit entities may misstate functional amounts to

- circumvent Internal Revenue Service requirements,
- comply with grant provisions or debt covenants,
- meet donor or grantor expectations with respect to program accomplishments, or
- minimize amounts reported as support expenses relating to fundraising and management and general expenses.

INTERNAL ACCOUNTING CONTROLS

As in the case with governmental entities, internal accounting controls are also of concern in not-for-profit entities. The internal control structure of many small- and medium-sized not-for-profit entities lacks the staff or lacks qualified staff in administrative or accounting and finance functions. This may result in improper segregation of duties, a high level of error in recording transactions, or missing or ineffective control systems.

Another unique aspect of not-for-profit entities with respect to the consideration of fraud is that of employee compensation and turnover. In many cases, employees of not-for-profit entities may be paid less than their counterparts in the private sector. This may be especially true for administrative or overhead type positions. As a result, employee turnover in these types of positions may be high when compared to private sector entities. These factors considered with limited administrative and accounting and finance functions represent textbook conditions for fraud.

REPEAT SIGNIFICANT DEFICIENCIES, MATERIAL WEAKNESSES, AND OTHER MATTERS RELATED TO INTERNAL CONTROL

Many of the internal control weaknesses discussed previously often result in significant deficiencies or material weaknesses. In not-for-profit entities, there may be a strong mindset toward providing services to achieve the mission of the organization at the expense of administrative support functions. As a result, deficiencies in internal control may continue to exist for a number of years. This may also hold true for other matters related to internal control repeated from year to year.

An auditor of a not-for-profit entity may need to consider these situations as fraud risk factors. The reasons for not implementing other matters related to internal control recommendations or not correcting significant deficiencies may indicate an attitude of rationalization throughout the entire not-for-profit entity. Additionally, the continued existence of missing or ineffective internal controls might create incentives or opportunities for fraud to occur.

SPLIT-INTEREST AGREEMENTS

Donors may enter into trust agreements or other arrangements wherein a not-for-profit entity may receive benefits that are shared with other organizations. Terms of these arrangements may be revocable by the donor in certain situations. These agreements may exist for either a finite number of years, in perpetuity, or for the remaining life of a specific individual.

Due to the number of estimates inherent in measuring assets and liabilities that exist in the typical split-interest agreement, a number of revenue recognition issues may exist. Such agreements are usually of the following types:

- Charitable lead trusts
- Perpetual trusts held by third parties
- Charitable remainder trusts
- Charitable gift annuities
- Pooled (life) income funds

The nature of a split interest agreement requires estimates in a number of areas including the following:

- Life expectancy of the donor and beneficiaries
- Types of investments to be made
- Investment returns
- Discount rates

Key Point

In both governmental and not-for-profit entities, management and those charged with governance are often focused on providing services rather than internal control. As such, repeat control deficiencies may indicate an attitude of rationalization throughout the entire organization. Additionally, the continued existence of missing or ineffective controls might create incentives or opportunities for fraud to occur.

KNOWLEDGE CHECK

3. Which is true of not-for-profit entities?

   a. Employees of not-for-profit entities are often paid less than their counterparts in the private sector.
   b. Employees of not-for-profit entities never feel pressured to appear efficient or effective in order to attract donors or to obtain grant funds.
   c. Not-for-profit entities have very low turnover in accounting and other support positions.
   d. Owners of a not-for-profit entity often pressure employees to do more with less.

Fraud Risks in Governmental and Not-for-Profit Entities

Fraud risks of primary interest to management of governmental and not-for-profit entities and their auditors include the following:

- Those represented by the fraud triangle
    - Incentive or pressure
    - Opportunity
    - Rationalization or attitude

- Revenue recognition
- Accounting estimates

INCENTIVE OR PRESSURE

Generally, employees of governmental organizations are under constant *pressure* to provide more and higher-quality services with fewer resources. When the economy is in decline, there is added pressure on governmental organizations to maintain current tax rates and user charges. This places pressure on management of governmental organizations to meet or improve upon budgeted amounts. An *incentive* to overstate revenues or to understate expenses or expenditures may be created by this pressure.

Similarly, when the economy is in decline, there is often added pressure on not-for-profit entities to provide additional services or the same services to a larger population. This may *pressure* the management of not-for-profit entities to meet or exceed service-level targets for both outputs and outcomes.

In an effort to obtain additional grant funds or contributions from resource providers, not-for-profit entities may have an *incentive* to overstate revenues or results. Additionally, not-for-profit entities may have an incentive to understate expenses in an effort to appear more efficient or effective to potential grantors or donors. For some higher levels of management, annual compensation may be based in part on the financial, service, or overall performance of the not-for-profit organization. This may create an incentive for fraud among those employees.

OPPORTUNITY

Lack of personnel or the lack of sufficiently qualified personnel may exist in administrative and accounting and finance functions in governmental and not-for-profit entities—especially smaller organizations. The resulting lack of, or ineffective, internal control creates *opportunities* for fraud.

Governmental organizations often have a number of locations taking cash in payment of services such as recreation centers, police departments, libraries, and the like. Lacking or ineffective controls create *opportunities* for fraud in these areas also. It is highly likely the amounts of many of these revenues are not material to the financial statements of the governmental organization taken as a whole. However, one of the objectives of financial reporting for governmental organizations is public accountability. Situations such as these, though not material to the financial statements, may be material when considered in the context of public accountability.

Not-for-profit entities may also be involved in a number of activities wherein large amounts of cash are collected. Additionally, cash may be collected in a number of locations or by persons lacking knowledge of existing internal controls. Lacking or ineffective controls create *opportunities* for fraud in these areas also. In some cases the amounts of these revenues may not be material to the financial statements of the not-for-profit entity taken as a whole. However, the objectives of financial reporting for not-for-profit entities may necessitate consideration of fraud programs and controls over these revenues.

Another characteristic of governmental organizations that may affect *opportunity* is the lack of anti-fraud programs and controls. Management in certain functions—such as the courts, judiciary, prison, and law enforcement—may believe anti-fraud programs and controls are unnecessary. A common misperception by management in these functions is that the nature of the function itself would deter anyone inclined to perpetrate fraud from working in these areas.

A somewhat similar attitude is often held by leadership and management of not-for-profit entities. They often view anti-fraud programs as "unfriendly" because they do not believe anyone would want to defraud a not-for-profit entity as it would decrease the resources that could be spent on mission-driven activities.

RATIONALIZATION OR ATTITUDE

Employees of governmental and not-for-profit entities are sometimes paid less than their counterparts in the private sector. This, coupled with the pressure to continue to provide a high level of service, may create an environment in which employees are able to *rationalize* perpetrating fraud. Some employees of governmental and not-for-profit entities may rationalize the misappropriation of organizational assets as compensation for their low, or perceived as low, salary levels. Again, such situations may not result in material misstatements of financial amounts. They are, however, violations of the public trust and serve as a measure of accountability.

REVENUE RECOGNITION AND ACCOUNTING ESTIMATES IN GOVERNMENTAL ORGANIZATIONS

Revenue Recognition

Because of the large number of grants or other intergovernmental revenues common to most governmental organizations, revenue recognition may be of particular concern with respect to fraud. The concern here is more with misstatements due to *fraudulent financial reporting* than misappropriation of assets. Generally accepted accounting principles related to recording exchange and non-exchange transactions contribute to the issue of proper revenue recognition in governmental organizations.

However, it is possible that in some governments revenue recognition may not be a fraud risk area from the perspective of *misappropriation of assets*. In some localities, all material revenues are received via electronic fund transfers or checks on a periodic basis from another governmental agency. This holds true for municipal property taxes in a number of states where the county acts as the tax assessor and collector for all taxing authorities within its jurisdiction. For many governments, revenues received in cash or at offsite locations with few internal controls are often immaterial to the financial statements taken as a whole.

Accounting Estimates

Accounting estimates made by governmental organizations are also of particular concern with respect to the consideration of fraud. From a fraudulent financial reporting perspective, the accounting estimates made by governmental organizations of primary concern relate to

- allowances for material uncollectible receivables such as taxes, special assessments, and customer receivables;
- estimated useful lives of capital assets;
- assessed condition of infrastructure assets if using the modified approach;
- actuarial valuations of pension and other post-employment benefit obligations;
- estimates of accrued compensated absences;
- estimated contingent liabilities for litigation, claims, and assessments;
- functional allocations of direct and indirect costs; and
- estimates and assumptions associated with determining fair value.

In addition to the areas noted previously, auditors of governmental organizations may also need to be concerned with how taxable property values are calculated for unique situations. For example, there may be no definitive statutory or acceptable alternative methodology for determining the assessed or taxable value of amusement parks, convention facilities, race tracks, and the like. The estimate of taxable value in these cases might be subject to manipulation, which could give rise to overstated property tax revenues and higher uncollectible taxes. In addition, the ability to manipulate taxable property values could give rise to the potential of collusion between the property tax assessor and the property owner in order to reduce the property tax burden for the property owner.

Estimates of budgeted revenues may also need to be reviewed by the auditor for potential manipulation as well as how they compare to actual results. It is not uncommon for governmental organizations to be overly optimistic in their revenue estimates or less than generous with expenditure allocations. In these cases, the auditor is primarily concerned with public accountability with respect to

- balanced budget requirements,
- the ability to continue to finance current services, and
- meeting bond and other debt obligations when due.

REVENUE RECOGNITION AND ACCOUNTING ESTIMATES IN NOT-FOR-PROFIT ENTITIES

Revenue Recognition

With respect to the consideration of fraud, revenue recognition may be of particular concern in not-for-profit entities. The concern here deals with misstatements due to both fraudulent financial reporting and misappropriation of assets.

Specifically, management of not-for-profit entities and their auditors may need to consider revenue recognition issues related to fraudulent financial reporting in the following areas:

- Contributions
- Membership dues
- Fundraising
- Split-interest agreements
- Grants

- Healthcare receivables
- Estimates and assumptions associated with determining fair value

Fraud risk associated with revenue recognition resulting from the misappropriation of assets relates primarily to the following areas:

- Cash receipts related to
    - contributions,
    - fees for services, and
    - dues.

Accounting Estimates

Accounting estimates made by not-for-profit entities are also of particular concern with respect to the consideration of fraud. From a fraudulent financial reporting perspective, the accounting estimates of concern made by not-for-profit entities relate to

- allowances for material uncollectible receivables such as pledges, special assessments, dues, and customer receivables;
- split-interest agreements;
- estimated useful lives of capital assets;
- estimates of accrued compensated absences;
- estimated contingent liabilities for litigation, claims, and assessments;
- allocation of joint costs; and
- functional allocations of expenses.

As in governmental organizations, it may be common for not-for-profit entities to be overly optimistic in their revenue estimates or less than generous with expense allocations. However, the legal level of budgetary accountability present in governmental organizations does not exist in not-for-profit entities. It is not uncommon for not-for-profit entities to "balance" projected expenses with unrealistic estimates of grant or contribution revenues. Therefore, auditors may need to understand the budgetary philosophy of the not-for-profit entity early in the planning stage of the audit.

KNOWLEDGE CHECK

4. Which is true of fraudulent financial reporting in governmental organizations?

    a. The accounting estimates made by governmental organizations do not include allowances for material uncollectible receivables such as taxes, special assessments, and customer receivables.
    b. The accounting estimates made by governmental organizations do not include functional allocations of direct and indirect costs.
    c. The accounting estimates made by governmental organizations include estimated useful lives of capital assets.
    d. Accounting estimates made by government engineers relating to the condition of infrastructure assets accounted for using the modified approach are not subject to management override.

Management Override

AU-C section 240, *Consideration of Fraud in a Financial Statement Audit* (AICPA, *Professional Standards*), requires the auditor to address the risk of, and respond to, management override of controls. The auditor's risk assessment and response to management override is required to be made separate from any conclusions regarding the existence of more specifically identifiable risks.

In every organization, management is in a unique position to perpetrate fraud because of the ability to

- Manipulate accounting records, and
- Prepare fraudulent financial statements by overriding controls that otherwise appear to operate effectively.

In many cases, this management is able to manipulate accounting records and financial statement information through the use of standard or "top down" journal entries (those made directly to records, such as spread sheets, used to prepare the financial statements rather than recorded in the books and records of the entity).

It's Possible...

Most business of governmental organizations is conducted in full view of the public. Therefore, it may appear that consideration of management override with respect to fraud requires little attention in audits of governmental organizations. However, because of the ease with which management may be able to access data and systems, and the reluctance of employees to discuss management abuses of such, it is an area of concern for the auditor.	Many not-for-profit entities in the United States are small to medium-sized entities and often are considered "closely held" due to limited turnover with the board of directors. As such, management may be able to access data and systems with relative ease. Regardless of the size of the not-for-profit entity, employees may be reluctant to discuss management abuses. For these reasons, management override is an area of concern for the auditor.

JOURNAL ENTRIES

Governmental and not-for-profit entities prepare journal entries of a routine nature throughout the reporting period and at the end of the fiscal period. As such, journal entries could be used by management of a governmental or not-for-profit entity to significantly affect amounts ultimately reported in the entity's financial statements.

With respect to journal entries, AU-C section 240 requires the auditor to understand the financial reporting process. This includes determining what reports are given to decision makers, the frequency of the reports, and how they are prepared. Auditors are also required to review procedures related to journal entries. In some governmental or not-for-profit entities, outdated financial management systems may necessitate manual entry of summary transaction data into a general ledger system. In some small or medium-sized governmental and not-for-profit entities, controls over journal entries may be missing or inadequate. This is due in many cases to a lack of adequately trained staff.

BUSINESS RATIONALE FOR SIGNIFICANT UNUSUAL TRANSACTIONS

Auditors are required to evaluate significant transactions that are unusual or outside the normal course of business. Because of the political nature of governmental organizations, the auditor might wish to focus on significant transactions that seem to be unusual in nature. Because of the potential for related-party transactions with usually well-meaning board members or with related regional or national affiliates, the auditor of a not-for-profit might wish to focus on significant unusual transactions. The lack of expertise or professional staff in small or medium-sized governmental and not-for-profit entities might unintentionally lead them into significant unusual transactions with potentially negative results.

With Respect to Governmental Organizations

With respect to governmental organizations, possible significant transactions and related auditor questions might include the following:

- *Economic development incentives*—Who ultimately benefits? Were multiyear projections used in the decision process? Were multiyear projections discounted to present value? Were discount rates reasonable? Were grant funds involved? Was the transaction predicated on performance objectives? Was the transaction arm's-length?
- *Onerous provisions in union contracts*—What negative impacts will be felt in other areas? Will this lead to other unions having the same expectations? Why were the concessions necessary?
- *Real estate purchases or sales*—Were permanent assets sold and, if so, why? What is the intended use for the proceeds of the sale? What is the intended use of the real estate purchased? Are environmental liabilities assumed or transferred? Was the real estate sold purchased in whole or in part with grant funds? Was the transaction arm's-length?
- *Land swaps*—What was the use of the land given up? What is the intended use of the land received? Are environmental liabilities assumed or transferred? Was the real estate sold purchased in whole or in part with grant funds? Was the transaction arm's-length?
- *Granting of easements*—What was the business purpose? Was it an exchange transaction and, if not, why? Was the transaction arm's-length?
- *Public and private partnerships*—Who ultimately benefits? Were multi-year projections used in the decision process? Were multi-year projections discounted to present value? Were discount rates reasonable? Was the transaction predicated on performance objectives? Was the transaction arm's-length?
- *Privatizing of governmental services*—Who ultimately benefits? Were multiyear projections used in the decision process? Were multiyear projections discounted to present value? Were discount rates reasonable? Were government-owned capital assets transferred to the new service provider and, if so, were any purchased with grant funds? Was the transaction predicated on performance objectives? Will service levels improve or remain unchanged? Does the transaction make business sense? Was the transaction arm's-length?
- *Early extinguishment of debt*—Was an economic benefit received? What benefit was received if no economic benefit was received? Was the transaction arm's-length?

With Respect to Not-for-Profit Entities

With respect to not-for-profit entities, possible significant transactions and related auditor questions might include the following:

- *Short- or long-term debt*—What was the purpose of the debt? Was the transaction made through the financial institution of a related party and, if so, was it arm's-length? What collateral or security interest was required to support the transaction?

- *Real estate purchases or sales*—Were permanent assets sold and if so, why? What is the intended use for the proceeds of the sale? What is the intended use of the real estate purchased? Are environmental liabilities assumed or transferred? Was the real estate sold purchased in whole or in part with grant funds? Was the real estate sold donated to the organization and, if so, do donor restrictions related to sale exist? Was the transaction arm's-length?
- *Public and private partnerships*—Who ultimately benefits? Were multiyear projections used in the decision process? Were multiyear projections discounted to present value? Were discount rates reasonable? Was the transaction predicated on performance objectives? Can the organization "opt out" with adequate notice? Was the transaction arm's-length?
- *Early extinguishment of debt*—Was an economic benefit received? What benefit was received if no economic benefit was received? Was the transaction arm's-length?

Key Point

 Professional standards require the auditor to consider management override as a fraud risk area. As such, the auditor is required to perform specific procedures related to journal entries and significant unusual transactions.

Planning Considerations in Audits of Governmental and Not-for-Profit Entities

The following areas may be of concern to the auditor of governmental and not-for-profit entities:

- *Availability and training of the firm's audit staff*
- *Exercise of professional skepticism*

Generally accepted government auditing standards require the audit engagement team to collectively possess the *knowledge and experience* to conduct an audit. As such, members of the audit engagement team are required to have a certain number of continuing education hours in governmental and not-for-profit accounting and auditing topics. Many states mirror these requirements or have adopted their own continuing education requirements for auditors of governmental or not-for-profit entities. As such, having adequate professional staff for governmental audit engagements may be a challenge for some audit firms—especially small audit firms.

This is a significant concern when considered in light of the AU-C section 200 requirement to exercise *professional skepticism*. It may be difficult for auditors to exercise the proper level of professional skepticism throughout an audit engagement when they have been on the engagement team for a number of years.

Summary

This chapter focused on the fraud risk areas that are unique to governmental and not-for-profit entities. In addition, this chapter discussed fraud risks in governmental and not-for-profit entities from the perspective of management as well as the auditor. Specific concerns relating to management override were also an area of focus in this chapter which included journal entries and the business rationale for transactions. Particular attention was given to those areas unique to governmental and not-for-profit entities.

Practice Questions

1. What are the three steps in the fraud process?

2. How does fraud risk related to incentives and pressure impact the consideration of fraud in a governmental organization?

3. How does fraud risk related to opportunity impact the consideration of fraud in a governmental organization?

4. Other than being required by AU-C section 240, why is revenue recognition of concern in an audit of a governmental organization?

5. List examples of accounting estimates of concern in the audit of a not-for-profit organization.

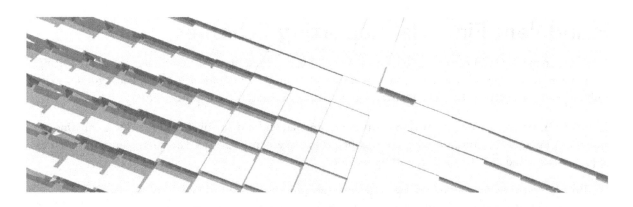

Chapter 5

FRAUD SCHEMES FOUND IN GOVERNMENTAL AND NOT-FOR-PROFIT ORGANIZATIONS

LEARNING OBJECTIVES

After completing this chapter, you should be able to do the following:

- Identify common ways in which fraudulent financial reporting and misappropriation of assets is perpetrated in governmental and not-for-profit entities.
- Identify fraudulent financial reporting schemes found in governmental and not-for-profit entities.
- Identify misappropriation-of-assets fraud schemes found in governmental and not-for-profit entities.

Fraudulent Financial Reporting Schemes

There are an almost infinite number of ways in which to perpetrate fraud through the financial reporting mechanism. A number of incentives and pressures, opportunities, and rationalizations and attitudes exist with respect to fraudulent financial reporting in governmental and not-for-profit entities.

These circumstances are exacerbated in many governmental and not-for-profit entities due to missing or ineffective internal controls, not the least of which is management override. The most common schemes to perpetuate fraudulent financial reporting include

- Premature *revenue recognition* or delayed revenue recognition, and
- Premature *expenditure and expense recognition* or delayed expense recognition.

PREMATURE REVENUE RECOGNITION OR DELAYED REVENUE RECOGNITION

Premature revenue recognition is most common in a for-profit entity. However, the existence of certain incentives/ pressures and rationalizations/ attitudes coupled with opportunities also make this a potential fraud risk area in governmental and not-for-profit entities. In governmental and not-for-profit entities, premature recognition of revenue overstates revenues as well as assets and net assets.

Delayed Revenue Recognition

More common to governmental and not-for-profit entities than in for-profit entities is the potential for delayed revenue recognition. It may seem odd that an organization would want to understate revenues of the current period. As with premature revenue recognition in governmental and not-for-profit entities, certain incentives/pressures and rationalizations/attitudes coupled with opportunities make delayed revenue recognition a potential fraud risk area.

Meeting budgeted amounts is critical in governmental entities and may play a crucial role in not-for-profit entities as well. In these cases, management may have an incentive either to recognize revenue prematurely or to delay recognition of revenue. If current-year revenue estimates have not been met, an incentive to prematurely recognize revenue may exist. Conversely, if budget levels for the current year have already been achieved, an incentive to move revenue from the current period into the subsequent period may exist.

PREMATURE EXPENSE RECOGNITION OR DELAYED EXPENSE RECOGNITION

Premature or delayed expense recognition goes hand-in-hand with premature or delayed revenue recognition. If a governmental or not-for-profit entity has an incentive or is pressured to meet certain revenue goals, the same incentives or pressures to meet expense goals may also exist.

Premature expense recognition is common in governmental and not-for-profit entities while virtually unheard of in for-profit entities. As with delayed revenue recognition, it may seem odd that an organization would want to overstate expenses of the current period. One of the most common reasons this may exist as a potential fraud risk in audits of not-for-profit entities, and is extremely common in audits of governmental organizations, relates to incentives, rationalizations, and attitudes in these organizations.

In many governmental organizations, appropriations that are not expended by year-end are lost. Having actual expenditures significantly less than appropriated amounts may negatively affect the amounts appropriated in subsequent years. This is a very common situation among governmental organizations and it has resulted in the "use it or lose it" mentality common among many of these organizations.

Fraudulent Financial Reporting Revenue Recognition

GENERAL ISSUES AND CONCERNS

Specific issues and concerns related to revenue recognition and the consideration of fraud in audits of governmental and not-for-profit entities include

- overstatement of earnings or increases in net assets or net position,
- fictitious revenues,
- improper application of revenue recognition principles,
- overstatement of assets, and
- understatement of allowances for receivables.

Potential Indicators of Fraudulent Financial Reporting Due to Revenue Recognition
*   Significant or unusual adjustments to receivables at or near year-end
*   Documentation relating to cash receipts is missing or altered
*   Cash flow from operating activities is inconsistent with actual cash flow
*   Significant or unusual entries to reconcile major revenue accounts
*   Unusual or unexplained significant fluctuations in major revenues from year to year or from budgeted amounts
*   Significant (in amount or frequency) related-party transactions
*   Revenue transactions that have been pre- or post-dated from the actual transaction date
*   Significant journal entries made to major revenue accounts rather than flowing through from adjustments made in subsidiary accounts

GOVERNMENTAL ORGANIZATIONS

With respect to the consideration of fraud, *revenue recognition* may be of particular concern in governmental organizations. In governmental organizations, revenue recognition is a function of the measurement focus and basis of accounting for a particular financial statement. As illustrated in the following table, there are several key areas where fraudulent financial reporting may occur through improper revenue recognition.

Areas Where Improper Revenue Recognition May Occur in Governmental Organizations
Nonexchange transactions
Grant revenues
Revenues of government type activities
Pledged revenues

Nonexchange Transactions

Classification and recognition criteria specified by generally accepted accounting principles create a number of areas where the potential for fraudulent financial reporting may occur with respect to nonexchange transactions. For example, the estimated time between the collection of local sales taxes by the vendor and the ultimate receipt of same at the local government level could be subject to a number of different interpretations. Additionally, the amount estimated to be recognized in this case could be calculated using several different assumptions. To properly address revenue recognition in relation to the consideration of fraud in financial statement audits of governmental organizations, the auditor will need to be aware of

- the types of non-exchange transactions that exist in the governmental organization,
- when revenues from each type of non-exchange transaction are available,
- measurement basis for each type of non-exchange transaction,
- all parties to the non-exchange transaction,
- the entity providing the resources and any contractual commitments associated therewith, and
- when the government has a legally enforceable right to claim the resources.

Grant Revenues

Because grants are *often nonexchange transactions*, the terms of a particular grant will dictate the recognition of assets, revenues, and expenses for purposes of financial statement reporting. However, from the perspective of fraudulent financial reporting, grant revenues provide an additional area of concern.

> In the case of *program-specific grants*, the governmental organization may feel pressure from the community to demonstrate the program sustained itself with grant revenues. As such, an aggressive approach to recording grant revenues and a soft line approach to grant expenses may be adopted by the governmental organization. Such an attitude may result in material misstatements in the financial statements. If the auditor observes such a situation and determines the misstatement was intentional, then there is evidence fraud may exist.

Revenues of Governmental Activities

For basic financial statements prepared at the government-wide level by the governmental organization, there may be a number of areas of concern that relate to revenues of governmental activities. Typically, a government makes day-to-day decisions based on fund level data and may, therefore, not be concerned with issues related to the full accrual basis of accounting with respect to governmental activities. Additionally, there may be little concern for whether functions generate functional net revenues or incur functional net expenses as reported in the government-wide financial statements. The government-wide measurement focus and basis of accounting required by GASB No. 34, *Basic Financial Statements—and Management's Discussion and Analysis—for State and Local Governments*, as amended, may result in intentional misstatements in the government-wide financial statements. As such, revenue recognition issues relate to

- proper identification of governmental and business-type activities,
- recognition of all material amounts representing full accrual transactions for governmental type activities in the government-wide statements,
- accuracy of amounts calculated or estimated representing adjustments to fund level amounts for full accrual transactions at the government-wide level,
- allocation of operating and capital grant revenues to the proper function, and
- determination of revenue sources representing charges for services and allocation of such to proper functions.

Pledged Revenues

Another area of concern with respect to fraudulent financial reporting and revenue recognition by governmental organizations relates to revenues pledged as security for long-term debt. In the case of long-term debt, bond covenants may require a certain level of revenues or specify certain minimum debt service coverage ratios. Governmental organizations may have an incentive in such cases to misstate revenues in order not to appear to be in violation of their bond covenants.

KNOWLEDGE CHECK

1. Which is typically NOT a significant area of concern regarding revenue recognition in governmental organizations?

    a. Exchange transactions.
    b. Grant revenues.
    c. Pledged revenues.
    d. Revenues of governmental activities.

NOT-FOR-PROFIT ENTITIES

With respect to the consideration of fraud, *revenue recognition* may be of particular concern in not-for-profit entities. As illustrated in the following table, there are several key areas where fraudulent financial reporting may occur through improper revenue recognition.

Areas Where Improper Revenue Recognition May Occur in Not-for-Profit Entities
🔑 Contributions
🔑 Membership dues
🔑 Fundraising
🔑 Split-interest agreements
🔑 Grants
🔑 Healthcare receivables

Analytical procedures related to revenue recognition that might prove helpful in evaluating the risk of material misstatement due to fraud might include

- comparing *significant changes in major revenue sources* and fundraising activities by type of resource provider with those of the prior year,
- reviewing *significant contributions by resource provider* and comparing them to those of the prior year, and
- comparing volume of *purchases by vendor for significant increases* from the prior year.

Contributions

Contributions are often significant to the total resources available to the not-for-profit entity. Often contributions consist of a donor promise to give which may be *subject to donor restrictions imposing time or use restrictions* either on a temporary or permanent basis. Such contributions are required to be classified as restricted assets until the restriction has been lifted or satisfied. Given the conditions of the fraud triangle, proper classification of contributions may be a fraud risk area for not-for-profit entities.

Contributions constituting *promises to give by related parties* may be of special concern with respect to fraudulent financial reporting. Many not-for-profit entities recruit board members and other key volunteers with the understanding they will "give or get" a certain amount of contributions for the not-for-profit entity. As such, these individuals may pledge generous contributions in the form of promises to give but may slowly pay these pledges. In some cases, pledges from board members and other key volunteers may go unpaid altogether. The policies of the not-for-profit entity with respect to estimating the uncollectible portion of pledges may be inadequate in these cases, which may result in material misstatements in the financial statements.

Another area of concern is whether proper determinations have been made as to whether promises to give are conditional or unconditional.

Membership Dues

As with trade receivables of a for-profit entity, receivables of not-for-profit entities for membership dues may represent a financial reporting fraud risk. Resources from membership dues and assessments may represent a significant resource for not-for-profit entities.

Members of not-for-profit entities may receive tangible or intangible benefits from their membership in the organization. Therefore, membership dues or assessments may represent *exchange or non-exchange transactions or be a combination* of both. Financial Accounting Standards Board (FASB) *Accounting Standards Codification* (ASC) Topic 958, *Not-for-Profit Entities*, delineates a number of indicators useful in determining the contribution and exchange portions of membership dues.

In *exchange transactions*, the not-for-profit entity must perform in order for the membership dues earnings process to be complete. For financial statement reporting, this may indicate the potential to report a portion of membership dues as deferred revenues. Improper determination of when the membership dues earnings process is complete may result in material misstatements in the financial statements of not-for-profit entities.

The auditor will need to be aware of the benefits, goods, services, and the like accruing to the member in order to determine whether membership dues represent an exchange or non-exchange transaction or a combination of both.

Audit procedures related to membership dues could involve analytical procedures using non financial information such as membership lists, attendance records, dues schedules, and newsletters. The risk of material misstatement of membership dues from fraud should be evaluated in light of the reliance to be placed on such non financial data.

Fundraising

Many not-for-profit entities conduct *special events* as fundraising or joint activities. Such activities may include dinners, theater parties, seminars, and conferences: and attendees may or may not receive a direct benefit.

For special events that are *peripheral or incidental activities* reporting such activities at net amounts (costs netted are limited to direct costs) is permitted by FASB ASC 958. However, if such activities are *ongoing major or central activities*, generally accepted accounting principles require revenues and expenses of these activities to be reported at gross amounts.

Accounting and financial reporting related to special fundraising or joint activities is somewhat complex and subjective. The options allowed under generally accepted accounting principles present a number of potential areas in which fraudulent financial reporting may occur. The determination of and accounting for revenues and expenses associated with special events require a thorough understanding of the event, its intended purpose, and the related costs to the not-for-profit entity as well as the benefits to the attendees.

Split-Interest Agreements

Donors may enter into trust agreements or other arrangements wherein a not-for-profit entity may receive benefits that are shared with others. Terms of these arrangements may be revocable by the donor in certain situations. These agreements may exist for either a finite number of years, in perpetuity, or for the remaining life of a specific individual. Such agreements include the following:

- Charitable lead trusts
- Perpetual trusts held by third parties
- Charitable remainder trusts
- Charitable gift annuities
- Pooled (life) income funds

Split-interest agreements present a number of revenue recognition issues for the not-for-profit entity. These issues include

- proper ownership of the assets and related earnings included in the split-interest agreement,
- proper valuation of the assets and related earnings included in the split-interest agreement, and
- proper valuation and recognition of the liabilities assumed under the split-interest agreement.

In order to determine the proper financial reporting of split-interest agreements, the auditor may find it helpful to answer the following questions:

- Is the split-interest agreement revocable by the donor?
- Does the not-for-profit have a lead or remainder interest in the split-interest agreement?
- Are there donor-imposed conditions in the split-interest agreement?
- Has the split-interest agreement been properly executed by all required parties?
- Does an unrelated third party act as agent or trustee?

- Does the third-party agent or trustee have variance power to redirect the benefits?
- Are the not-for-profit entity's rights to benefits conditional?
- Is income earned on the assets held under the split-interest agreement available to the not-for-profit entity and, if so, is it available for use without donor-imposed restrictions?
- Can the fair value of the split-interest agreement be objectively determined?
- Was the discount rate applied in estimating fair value objectively determined and consistently applied?
- Does the split-interest agreement include an embedded derivative subject to the measurement provisions of FASB ASC 815?
- Have assets and liabilities recognized under split-interest agreements been properly disclosed in the financial statements and the notes?

Grants

Because of the large number of grants common to many not-for-profit entities, *revenue recognition* may be of particular concern with respect to fraudulent financial reporting. Generally, the terms of the particular grant will dictate the recognition of revenues and expenses for purposes of financial statement reporting.

Not-for-profit entities feeling pressure to generate positive operating results may take an aggressive approach to recording grant revenues and a soft line approach to grant expenses. Such an attitude may result in material misstatements in the financial statements. If the auditor observes such a situation and determines the misstatement was intentional, then there is evidence fraud may exist.

KNOWLEDGE CHECK

2. Which is typically NOT a significant area of concern regarding revenue recognition in not-for-profit entities?

   a. Fundraising.
   b. Charges for services.
   c. Grants.
   d. Membership dues.

Healthcare Receivables

Additional concerns related to revenue recognition and fraudulent financial reporting by not-for-profit healthcare organizations exist with respect to reimbursements from insurers and government sponsored healthcare programs. The knowing misstatement of facts that results in unfair material profit through medical coverage may constitute fraud.

False claims by physicians, hospitals, and other healthcare providers may result in overstated revenues, receivables, or both. Ways in which false claims may result in material misstatements in the financial statements include the following:

- *Misstatement of services rendered or goods provided*—Goods or services are never given or given at lesser levels than indicated on claims filed with insurers, for example.
- *Upcoding*—Claims contain more expensive products or services than the products or services actually provided.

- *Unbundling services*—Involves splitting charges for a comprehensive procedure with one all-inclusive charge into individual procedures or services with collectively higher charges.
- *Provision of unnecessary treatment*—Services actually rendered that are unnecessary to the proper treatment of the diagnosed illness or condition.
- *Kickbacks*—Illegal incentives provided by vendors to healthcare providers (individuals or organizations) for the performance of a service.

Fraudulent Financial Reporting Functional and Fund Classifications

GENERAL ISSUES AND CONCERNS

Key Point

There are a number of areas where the requirements of generally accepted accounting principles may be intentionally misapplied by governmental or not-for-profit entities in order to meet expectations of the users of their respective financial statements.

The functional classification of expenditures and expenses is unique to financial reporting by governmental and not-for-profit entities. Often the object or natural classification of a transaction is electronically allocated to pre-determined functions through the "black box" of an entity's financial management system.

Misstatements of expenditures and expenses within functions will not, in all likelihood, affect the overall change in net position or net assets for a given period. However, expense ratios may be important to both governmental and not-for-profit entities. This incentive, coupled with the "black box" aspect of functional allocations, increases the risk of material misstatements, whether intentional or fraudulent, in audits of governmental and not-for-profit entities.

With respect to premature or delayed expense recognition, typical situations or circumstances that may indicate the existence of fraudulent financial reporting related thereto include

- significant or unusual adjustments to payables at or near year-end,
- documentation relating to cash disbursements or accounts payable is missing or altered,
- cash flow used in operating activities is inconsistent with actual cash flow,
- significant or unusual entries to reconcile major liability or expense accounts,
- unusual or unexplained significant fluctuations in major liabilities or expenses from year to year or from budgeted amounts,
- significant (in amount or frequency) related-party transactions,
- payable or expense transactions that have been pre- or post-dated from the actual transaction date, and
- significant journal entries made to major liability or expense accounts rather than flowing through from adjustments to subsidiary accounts.

GOVERNMENTAL ORGANIZATIONS

Use of the fund structure provides a mechanism by which governmental organizations may be able to conceal, misrepresent, or manipulate transactions whether with the intent to defraud or not. Many governmental officials and employees find it easy to rationalize improper fund transactions or accounting for a number of reasons including the following:

- Maintains current tax levels
- Maintains current user fee levels
- The belief that no one understands fund accounting

- The belief that all financial resources should be available for all operations of the governmental organization regardless of external restrictions

Interfund transactions can conceal a number of irregularities and may result in fraudulent financial reporting if not detected. Examples of potentially fraudulent transactions include

- offsetting operating losses in business-type activities,
- concealing budget shortfalls, and
- infusing working capital to meet bond covenant ratios.

GASB Statement No. 34, as amended, requires a number of disclosures related to reciprocal and nonreciprocal interfund transactions. These required disclosures may affirm there are no material misstatements or they may represent areas where the potential risk of material misstatements due to fraud may exist.

In the statement of activities, GASB Statement No. 34, as amended, requires the reporting of expenses at the government-wide level by functional classification. Functional expenses are offset by specifically identifiable grants (operating and capital) and charges for services in the government-wide level statement of activities, but not offset at the fund level. At the governmental fund level, expenditures are also presented within functional, rather than natural, classifications. Some governmental agencies may misstate functional amounts to circumvent legal requirements or to comply with grant provisions or bond covenants.

NOT-FOR-PROFIT ENTITIES

Under the requirements of FASB ASC 958, not-for-profit *voluntary health and welfare entities* report expenses by their functional and natural classifications in a matrix format. *Other not-for-profit entities* are required to report expenses by functional classifications and are encouraged to provide information about their natural expense classification.

Some not-for-profit entities may misstate functional amounts to circumvent Internal Revenue Service requirements or to comply with grant provisions or debt covenants. In some cases, not-for-profit entities may misstate revenues by net asset classification in order to appear to have met matching requirements of grants or other donor-imposed restrictions.

For many potential resource providers, the *expense ratios* of not-for-profit entities play an important role in their decision to contribute to the organization. Potential resource providers want to know if their contributions will be used in furtherance of the organization's mission or for administrative or fundraising purposes.

Allocation of *fundraising expenses* is an area that represents a potential fraud risk with respect to financial reporting. Generally accepted accounting principles require all fundraising costs be expensed when incurred. Such accounting treatment is required regardless of the period in which contributions resulting from these efforts will be received. Not-for-profit entities may misstate changes in net assets by capitalizing fundraising expenses rather than recognizing an expense when they are incurred.

Accounting for Joint Activities

If the criteria of purpose, audience, and content are met, the costs of a joint activity that are identifiable with a particular function should be charged to that function and joint costs should be allocated between fundraising and the appropriate program or management and general function. If any of the criteria are not met, all costs of the joint activity should be reported as fundraising costs, including costs that otherwise might be considered program or management and general costs if they had been incurred in a different activity, subject to the exception in the following sentence. Costs of goods or services provided in exchange transactions that are part of joint activities, such as costs of direct donor benefits of a special event (for example, a meal), should not be reported as fundraising. FASB ASC 958 discusses the accounting and reporting requirements related to joint costs.

Like special events, the determination of and accounting for costs of joint activities requires a thorough understanding of the activity as well as the mission and operations of the not-for-profit entity. As such, this area may well represent a significant risk of material financial statement misstatement.

Misappropriation of Assets Overview

Misappropriation of assets is commonly referred to as theft or defalcation and involves the actual theft of an entity's assets. In the consideration of fraud in financial statement audits, the effect of theft results in material misstatements in the financial statements. Individuals involved in the theft of publicly owned assets belonging or entrusted to a governmental organization may face civil or criminal charges if caught. Thefts of assets owned by not-for-profit entities may carry the same penalties, especially if such assets were purchased with government financial assistance.

> **Assets Subject to Misappropriation in Governmental and Not-for-Profit Entities**
>
> - Cash
> - Cash equivalents, such as food stamps, tuition vouchers, and lottery tickets, either processed or kept as inventory
> - Legally confiscated items
> - Inventories of supplies, etc., and physical assets that are
>
>   - small in size,
>   - high in value,
>   - high in consumer demand,
>   - easily convertible to cash, and
>   - lacking in ownership identification
>
> - Equipment that is subject to personal or non-program use, such as cellular phones, digital cameras, computers, vehicles, tools, etc.
> - Physical assets susceptible to personal use or redirection, such as unused or out-of-the-way buildings, vacant land, obsolete equipment, or abandoned assets

GENERAL ISSUES AND CONCERNS

The theft of assets typically occurs in a number of ways, including

- *embezzlement* of receipts including skimming;
- *stealing* assets; or
- causing an entity to *pay for goods or services that have not been received* through credit card abuse, fictitious vendors, payroll schemes, subrecipient fraud, conflicts of interest, or other schemes.

Misappropriation of assets is often accomplished by circumventing controls and may be accompanied by

- *false records or documents, or*
- *misleading records or documents.*

Because of the public nature of governmental and not-for-profit entities, the misappropriation of assets may have a more far-reaching impact than if such defalcations occurred in a for-profit entity. Public response to fraud in governmental and not-for-profit entities may be extremely negative regardless of the monetary amount of the theft or defalcation. Therefore, the potential impact of theft and defalcations in governmental and not-for-profit entities may be significant without being material to the financial statements taken as a whole.

In many governmental and not-for-profit entities an *attitude* may be present that encourages employees to use assets of the organization for their personal gain. This may be as insignificant as management turning a blind eye to use of copiers for personal use or as egregious as operating a personal business from the fire station. Though such situations may not result in material misstatements due to the misappropriation of assets, they are, however, violations of the public trust.

Effective methods by which the auditor may evaluate whether misappropriation of assets might indicate material misstatements due to fraud include

- *analytical procedures* conducted as substantive procedures as part of the overall review stage of the audit, and
- *brainstorming sessions* with all members of the audit engagement team at or near the end of the engagement to discuss the magnitude and collective significance of any such observations.

Analytical procedures are often effective in detecting material misstatements due to misappropriation of assets. The following analytical procedures may be appropriate in audits of *both governmental and not-for-profit entities*:

- Ascertain if any *significant budget adjustments* were made at, near, or after year-end.
- Determine whether all budget adjustments made at, near, or after year-end were properly and timely *approved by the governing body*, if required.
- Compare volume of *purchases by vendor for significant increases* to the prior year.
- Review *adjustments to perpetual fixed asset inventory records* based on current year physical counts.
- Compare prior year and current year activity for number and amount of write-offs for
  - significant *bank reconciling items*;
  - significant *uncollectible receivables*;
  - significant *supplies inventory* adjustments; and
  - significant *sales of property, plant, and equipment*.
- Review *significant transfers between classes of net assets and net position* made at, near, or after year-end (not-for-profit entities).
- Ascertain *disposition of physical assets donated* to the organization during the current year.

Key Point

There are a number of analytical procedures that may be performed in audits of governmental and not-for-profit entities that might prove helpful in determining whether fraud due to misappropriation of assets has occurred.

KNOWLEDGE CHECK

3. Which analytical procedures would NOT be appropriate in audits of governmental and not-for-profit entities?

    a. Ascertain if any significant budget adjustments were made at, near, or after year-end.
    b. Review significant transfers between classes of net assets and net position made at, near, or after year-end.
    c. Comparing gains and losses on sales of capital assets for the current year to the prior year.
    d. Comparing volume of *purchases by vendor for significant increases* to the prior year

Misappropriation of Assets Common Fraud Schemes

As with fraudulent financial reporting, there are an almost infinite number of ways in which to perpetrate fraud through the misappropriation of assets. As discussed previously, a number of incentives and pressures, opportunities, and rationalizations and attitudes exist with respect to fraud through the misappropriation of assets in governmental and not-for-profit entities.

These circumstances are exacerbated in many governmental and not-for-profit entities due to missing or ineffective internal controls, not the least of which is management override. The most common schemes to perpetrate fraud due to misappropriation of assets are discussed in detail in the following sections. Included is fraud due to misappropriation of assets in the following areas:

Embezzlement of cash receipts and fraudulent disbursements (including accounts receivable frauds)	Personnel frauds	Diversion of physical assets including property, plant, and equipment
Procurement & contracting frauds	*Common Schemes to Misappropriate Assets*	Diversion of program benefits and assets

Misappropriation of Assets Common Fraud Schemes Procurement and Contracting

GENERAL ISSUES AND CONCERNS

Onerous procurement and contracting requirements exist in most governmental entities. Such procedures and requirements may exist in not-for-profit entities to a lesser degree. Procurement and contractor fraud have been identified as the two most significant and costly types of fraud in government organizations. Whether intentional or not, it is the taxpayer who pays when governmental organizations are the victims of procurement or contract scams. In not-for-profit organizations, it is the individual donor or government grantor that bears the cost of such fraud.

Common indicators of the potential for the misappropriation of assets due to procurement or contracting fraud include the following:

- Unusual vendor names and addresses
- Copies of invoices, purchase orders, or receiving documents rather than original documentation
- Orders for materials or supplies already on hand in sufficient quantities or that are scheduled for disposal or whose use will be discontinued due to obsolescence
- Orders for materials or supplies not consistent with the operations or mission of the government or not-for-profit organization
- Delivery addresses different from the purchaser's physical locations
- Purchases falling just below the threshold for required next-level approval (in quantity or amount)
- Split purchases using purchase orders, vendor invoices, change orders, and the like
- Payments to vendors not on approved vendor lists
- Signature of management or supervisory personnel on documents typically signed by subordinate personnel
- Suppliers or contractors receiving significant amounts of business from the organization
- Prices in excess of market or expected market especially when large quantities are ordered
- Complaints from vendors or suppliers regarding not being allowed to bid, stringent bid specifications or procedures, or inadequate time allowed for responding to bid requests
- Contract award patterns that may indicate bids are being rotated
- Low quality combined with high prices including high product failure or return rates
- Sole source procurements in significant number or without adequate justification

Procurement

A number of controls related to procuring goods and services may be in place in governmental or not-for-profit entities. Unfortunately, the lack of adequate numbers of sufficiently competent administrative or finance staff significantly affects the effectiveness of procurement controls. Ideally, procurement controls typically ensure purchases are made

- for approved purposes,
- in reasonable quantities,
- at competitive prices, and
- from qualified and reputable vendors.

The use of procurement cards by governmental and not-for-profit entities has increased significantly in recent years. Procurement cards minimize the burden of tedious purchasing controls and requirements and eliminate administrative paperwork as well. Therefore, a growing number of governmental and not-for-profit entities are using procurement cards for routine or small purchases. Unfortunately, not all governmental and not-for-profit entities have effective controls in place to ensure proper use of these purchasing cards.

Contracting

Generally, governmental and not-for-profit entities enter into contracts covering an extended time period or involving significant amounts of human, capital, or financial resources. As such, stringent controls and procedures similar to those existing over the regular procurement of goods and services may exist in governmental and not-for-profit entities. Unfortunately, as with procurement procedures and controls, the lack of adequate numbers of sufficiently competent administrative or finance staff significantly affects the effectiveness of contracting controls.

Controls governing contracting by governmental and not-for-profit entities are typically designed to eliminate the following:

- *Bribery* in the contract
- *Collusion* among
    - contractors,
    - the contractor and the governmental or not-for-profit entity, and
    - the contractor and employees of the governmental or not-for-profit entity

- *False or double billing*
- *False certification of quality* of parts or test results
- *Substitution of parts*, imitation, or otherwise inferior

GOVERNMENTAL ORGANIZATIONS

Controls and procedures related to procurement and contracting by governmental organizations are usually more prevalent and more effective than those found in not-for-profit entities.

In most governmental organizations, procurement and contracting procedures constitute legal requirements. These legal requirements may address such areas as

- goods or services requiring a competitive bid or proposal process,
- dollar thresholds requiring a competitive bid or proposal process,
- dollar thresholds requiring a certain number of verbal or written quotes,
- specific vendors not qualified to provide goods or services to governmental organizations within a certain jurisdiction,
- the number and content of required legal notices or advertisements for requested bids or proposals,
- the lowest level at which bids or contracts may be awarded to successful bidders or proposers, and
- the definition of related parties for specific types of governmental organizations.

Violations of such procurement or contracting requirements may equate to breaking the law and therefore be subject to civil or criminal prosecution. Procurement or contracting procedures and requirements may be mandated by any or all of the following:

- State statutes
- Local ordinance
- Local resolution
- Local approved or adopted policy

NOT-FOR-PROFIT ENTITIES

Controls and procedures related to procurement and contracting by not-for-profit entities are usually less prevalent and may be less stringent than those found in governmental organizations. However, with respect to expenditures of funds received under federal or other governmental financial assistance programs, not-for-profit entities may be required to meet procurement or contracting procedures that exceed their own internally adopted policies.

Related-party transactions represent another area wherein misappropriation of assets may occur in not-for-profit entities. These types of transactions may be especially prevalent in small to medium-sized not-for-profit entities or in those organizations with loose, missing, or ineffective controls over procurement and contracting.

Misappropriation of Assets Common Fraud Schemes Cash Receipts and Fraudulent Disbursements

GENERAL ISSUES AND CONCERNS

As with for-profit entities, an opportunity for the misappropriation of assets exists in governmental and not-for-profit entities whenever cash is collected at or disbursed from a number of locations. Also of concern in the consideration of fraud with respect to cash receipts and disbursements is the effectiveness of controls over disbursement transactions initiated at offsite locations.

Many of the concerns associated with the consideration of fraud with respect to cash receipts and disbursements relate to missing or ineffective controls. Because administrative and finance and accounting personnel in governmental and not-for-profit entities are often limited in number or expertise, this is of special concern for these organizations.

	Common Fraud Indicators of Misappropriation of Cash, Accounts Receivable, and Inventories
Cash Receipts and Disbursements	▪ Missing or out-of-sequence blank checks ▪ Significant bank reconciling items without reasonable explanation ▪ Second payee or unusual endorsements on checks ▪ Missing cancelled checks ▪ Unusual disbursement transactions or transactions lacking sufficient supporting documentation ▪ Citizen or customer complaints about amounts they owe the organization (for taxes, services rendered, contribution pledges, and the like)
Accounts Receivable	▪ Unexplained differences noted on receivable confirmations received ▪ Significant or unusual adjustments to receivable records ▪ Amounts deposited that are inconsistent with amounts due ▪ Significant credit balances in receivable accounts
Inventories	▪ Significant inventory shrinkage ▪ Unusual inventory turnover ▪ Significant unusual or unexplained entries to control or subsidiary inventory records ▪ Significant unusual or unexpected relationships in inventory and inventory related ratios ▪ Receiving reports differing from purchase orders, contracts, or vendor invoices

GOVERNMENTAL ORGANIZATIONS

Governmental organizations often receive cash at a number of locations, such as courthouses, recreation centers, police departments, utility departments, libraries, health clinics, and the like. The lack of sufficient support staff at these offsite locations exacerbates the effect of lacking or ineffective controls that may exist at these locations. A number of *opportunities* for the misappropriation of assets may be present in these locations.

Due to relative materiality, it is possible that in some governments, diversion of cash receipts may not be a fraud risk area from the perspective of misappropriation of assets. However, one of the objectives of financial reporting for governmental organizations is public accountability. Situations such as these, though not material to the financial statements, are material to public accountability.

NOT-FOR-PROFIT ENTITIES

Fraud through the misappropriation of cash may be of particular concern in not-for-profit entities. More prevalent than in governmental organizations is the lack of sufficient support staff at offsite locations of not-for-profit entities. In addition, not-for-profit entities often utilize volunteers in administrative or fundraising activities. These volunteers may be responsible for collecting large amounts of cash. This type of situation, together with generally lacking or ineffective controls, creates a number of *opportunities* for the misappropriation of assets in not-for-profit entities.

Though they are not cash receipts or disbursements, *services contributed* to or on behalf of not-for-profit entities might also be subject to misdirection or inappropriate utilization. Employees at certain levels of a not-for-profit entity might be in a position to ask the donor of professional services to also perform similar services for them personally. Contributed trade-type services such as electrical, plumbing, or HVAC are often actually performed by line-level employees rather than the person committing their organization to providing such services. In these cases, there is an increased opportunity for redirection of these services for the personal use of employees of the not-for-profit entity.

KNOWLEDGE CHECK

4. Which is true of cash receipts and fraudulent disbursements?

    a. Unlike for-profit entities, an opportunity for the misappropriation of assets does not exist in governmental and not-for-profit entities whenever cash is collected at or disbursed from a number of locations.

    b. Of concern in the consideration of fraud with respect to cash receipts and disbursements is the effectiveness of controls over disbursement transactions initiated at offsite locations.

    c. None of the audit concerns associated with the consideration of fraud with respect to cash receipts and disbursements relate to missing or ineffective controls.

    d. Limited administrative and finance and accounting personnel in governmental and not-for-profit entities are never a concern associated with the consideration of fraud with respect to cash receipts and disbursements.

Misappropriation of Assets Common Fraud Schemes Personnel Costs

GENERAL ISSUES AND CONCERNS

Governmental and not-for-profit entities primarily provide services rather than produce goods. Accordingly, a *significant amount of expenditures and expenses* in these organizations relate to personnel costs. In this matter, as with other fraud risk areas, the lack of adequate or sufficiently knowledgeable administrative or finance and accounting staff may result in lacking or ineffective controls.

As discussed previously, employees of governmental and not-for-profit entities are *typically paid less* than their counterparts in the private sector. To compensate, they may add hours to their time sheets that were not actually worked. At certain levels of management, if controls are missing, ineffective, or capable of override, it may be possible to create "fictitious employees."

Personnel Costs and the Fraud Triangle

In addition to historically lower salary levels, employees of governmental or not-for-profit entities are *subject to layoffs or reduced hours* when resources are insufficient to maintain existing services. Workforce reductions may also occur when significant grant funds are discontinued and alternative funding is not available to continue the program. This unstable work environment in governmental and not-for-profit entities may

- *pressure* employees to work another job while on the clock for the governmental or not-for-profit entity or
- create *incentives* for employees to look for ways to misappropriate assets either through the personnel system or other venues.

Common indicators of the potential for the misappropriation of assets due to personnel fraud include the following:

- Unusual or second-party endorsements on payroll checks
- Employees without the usual withholdings related to employer provided or offered benefits (such as insurance, retirement, or savings bonds)
- Missing, unusual-looking, or altered time and attendance records in general or frequently for the same employee(s)
- Time and attendance records signed by someone other than the usual supervisor in general or frequently for the same employee(s)

Exempt and Not-Exempt Employees

The issue of *classifying employees as exempt or not exempt* from Department of Labor regulations is often an issue in governmental and not-for-profit entities. This is especially true in most small and many medium-sized governmental or not-for-profit entities.

Classifying an employee as exempt when their essential duties do not meet federal guidelines for such classification results in the employee being underpaid with respect to overtime hours worked. When employees are classified as not exempt when their essential duties do not meet federal guidelines for such classification results in employees being overpaid with respect to overtime hours worked. These situations, if intentional and material, result in fraud with respect to the audits of the financial statements of governmental and not-for-profit entities. Material misstatements in the financial statements relate to both financial reporting and the misappropriation of assets.

In these situations, misstatements in financial reporting occur due to contingent liabilities related to underpaying employees, including the following:

- *Unpaid overtime and related benefits*—Including social security and Medicare, pension or retirement matching contributions, unemployment taxes, and the like
- *Penalties and interest*—Including those assessed by federal, state, and/ or local regulatory authorities

When employees are overpaid due to being incorrectly classified as not exempt from overtime regulations, assets of the governmental or not-for-profit entity are misappropriated. Employment-related benefits calculated on gross pay will also result in misappropriated assets. This situation is exacerbated if employees are reporting overtime hours for hours they did not actually work.

Hiring Procedures and Controls

Hiring procedures and controls in governmental and not-for-profit entities may create opportunities for fraud due to the misappropriation of assets. Governmental or not-for-profit entities may or may not be aware of the myriad of federal and state regulations governing hiring, paying, and disciplining employees. Again, the *lack of qualified administrative or finance and accounting personnel* typically contribute to missing or ineffective controls in these areas also.

Because of the generally *less than market wages* paid to employees of governmental and not-for-profit entities, applicants may overstate their qualifications in order to be paid more or to be hired in higher-level positions. Lower wages may also discourage qualified applicants and attract applicants with questionable backgrounds or those who may lack experience or legal resident status. This may be especially apparent in areas such as road, building, or grounds maintenance in governmental organizations, and in custodial, childcare, or food service positions in not-for-profit entities. Intentional avoidance of prudent hiring and screening procedures may represent a fraud risk area in financial statement audits of governmental and not-for-profit entities.

GOVERNMENTAL ORGANIZATIONS

As stated in the previous section, Department of Labor regulations require overtime pay for hours worked in excess of the standard workweek. In for-profit entities the standard workweek is typically considered to be 40 hours. For governmental organizations the standard workweek *may* be something other than 40 hours for a significant number of employees. Such employee groups typically include the following:

- *Public safety employees*—Law enforcement, corrections, fire, and rescue
- *Public health*—Staff at public hospitals and clinics, medical examiners, and the like
- *Public works*—Utility plant operators, road crews, building maintenance, and the like

When the number of hours in a standard workweek is purported to be something other than 40, management and auditors should be aware of the precedents that support the standard hours used for each employee group. When no legal precedent exists to support the standard hours used by the governmental organization, a misappropriation of assets may have occurred (employees overpaid) or contingent liabilities may exist (employees underpaid).

Paid overtime may create a material incentive for employees to misappropriate assets through manipulation of the control system. For example, fire personnel in local government organizations typically work a 24-hour shift and then are off duty for the next 48 hours. In this situation, there are usually 56 standard hours in the workweek, but because the end of the workweek or pay period spans two different days, overtime hours *may* be considered in the context of a 2- or 3-week period. When other fire personnel are ill, on vacation, or participating in training, it is necessary to replace them with other qualified fire personnel in order to maintain mandated minimum staffing levels. The result is that fire personnel often work several 24-hour overtime shifts in any given pay period.

Doing the math, it is easy to see that a number of 24-hour shifts at overtime rates may quickly create a material financial statement effect. When fire personnel work in collusion with each other to "take vacation" or "call in sick," fraud due to misappropriation of assets may be present. Auditors need to be cognizant of the potential for fraud due to these types of circumstances. An effective audit procedure in these circumstances is to compare annual W-2 earnings by employees to adopted compensation levels for their respective positions. Variances can then be reviewed for reasonableness. Budget to actual comparisons are also effective.

Again, it is important for management and auditors to understand the individual laws in this area for the particular location they are working in. Information can be obtained from the Department of Labor (www.dol.gov) and the state and local regulatory bodies where the client is located.

Key Point

 The inherent nature of public safety services provided by governmental organizations may create fraud risks that could result in the government incurring significant additional personnel costs.

NOT-FOR-PROFIT ENTITIES

With respect to the consideration of fraud in financial statement audits of not-for-profit entities personnel administration is significant because

- personnel costs are typically material to the financial statements taken as a whole,
- conditions related to the receipt of federal (or other government) financial assistance require prudence in personnel administration,
- amounts reimbursable under federal contracts or programs may be erroneously stated due to lacking or ineffective personnel controls and procedures, and
- improper applicant screening may result in wrongly placing dishonest employees in positions having access to assets susceptible to misappropriation.

Misappropriation of Assets Common Fraud Schemes Property, Plant, and Equipment

GENERAL ISSUES AND CONCERNS

Generally, property, plant, and equipment subject to misappropriation in governmental and not-for-profit entities includes physical assets that are

- small in size;
- high in value;
- high in consumer demand;
- easily convertible to cash;
- lacking in ownership identification;
- subject to personal or non-program use (such as cellular phones, digital cameras, computers, vehicles, or tools); or
- susceptible to personal use or redirection (such as unused or out-of-the way buildings, vacant land, obsolete equipment, or abandoned assets).

Misappropriation of physical assets may occur through

- stealing the assets or
- causing the entity to pay for goods or services that have not been received or that do not meet required specifications.

The misappropriation of physical assets is often accomplished by circumventing controls and may be accompanied by

- false records or documents or
- misleading records or documents.

In addition to the consideration of controls related to procurement, contracting, and cash disbursements, physical controls over property, plant, and equipment need to be considered as well. Physical controls need to be evaluated with respect to the potential for fraud due to misappropriation of the physical assets of the governmental or not-for-profit entity.

GOVERNMENTAL ORGANIZATIONS

Unauthorized Use

One of the primary concerns in audits of governmental organizations related to physical assets is determining if they were used inappropriately. This includes redirecting the use of physical assets to another government function or for personal gain.

In the case of assets wholly or partially acquired or constructed with federal financial assistance, redirecting the use of such assets may have significant repercussions. Often these physical assets may be used only for purposes specifically included in the grant agreement. Therefore, if the use of such an asset is to be redirected to another bona fide governmental function, permission of the grantor may be required in advance. Without such permission, provisions of the original grant agreement may require the governmental organization to return ownership and control of the asset to the granting agency. If unintentional, redirections of this type would not appear to result in a fraudulent transaction.

Assets confiscated in law enforcement activities are often allowed under some state statutes to be redirected for the use of law enforcement. Typically, these assets are allowed to be used in the edification or enhancement of specific or any law enforcement activities. Unfortunately, assets confiscated in law enforcement are often subject to inappropriate misappropriation—the results of which are usually seen on the evening news.

It may be difficult to design efficient and effective audit procedures to detect the misappropriation of publicly owned physical assets for personal use or gain. In many cases, the auditor may need to rely on internal controls to provide assurance related to the proper use of publicly owned physical assets.

Inquiry of appropriate personnel within the governmental organization may provide sufficient audit evidence related to the appropriate use of physical assets. However, it may be necessary for the auditor to design additional audit procedures. One procedure to consider is the observation of physical assets in use during scheduled work hours within and throughout the jurisdiction of the governmental organization. These observations could be compared to the "official" policies related to use with discrepancies discussed with appropriate client personnel. From these follow-up discussions, the auditor may be able to ascertain management's "attitude" regarding personal use of publicly owned assets, whether considered *de minimis* or flagrantly abusive.

KNOWLEDGE CHECK

5. Which is true of assets confiscated in law enforcement activities?

    a. Such assets may typically be used in the edification or enhancement of specific or any law enforcement activities.
    b. All confiscated assets revert to the state in which they were confiscated.
    c. Assets confiscated are not the type of assets that are subject to misappropriation.
    d. Misappropriation of assets confiscated in law enforcement activities is never of concern to the public.

Periodic Physical Inventory

Many states mandate an annual physical inventory of and accounting for the property, plant, and equipment owned by local governments. In many cases, a certain dollar threshold for this inventory and accounting is stated in the enabling legislation.

Local governmental organizations may also have their own adopted policies and procedures related to accounting for property, plant, and equipment. Such local policies and procedures may exceed the requirements of state mandates in some cases. Even though a periodic accounting of physical assets may be state mandated or locally required, it may not occur.

Some local governments lack adequate personnel to effectively administer a property control function or to conduct an annual inventory of their physical assets. In other governmental organizations, adequate personnel may exist to affect a property control function but the attitude of the organization precludes minimal efforts (annual inventory) of control.

The auditor would ascertain the reasons a governmental organization does not conduct at least an annual inventory of and accounting for its physical assets, whether mandated or not. These reasons would be evaluated in light of the potential fraud risk associated with the misappropriation of physical assets.

Identification and Control Systems

A common control technique to account for physical assets owned by governmental organizations is to "tag" the asset with some sort of a permanent tag or marking. The tag may show the inventory control number alone or additional information such as location, manufacturer, date acquired, maintenance schedule, and the like.

Obviously the effectiveness of a "tag" system will vary from one governmental organization to another. The auditor will need to evaluate the effectiveness of any tag systems in light of the fraud risk associated with the misappropriation of physical assets.

Sales and Disposals

Governmental organizations typically have stringent controls and legal requirements related to the sale or disposition of publicly owned physical assets. Unfortunately, lacking or ineffective controls often exist with respect to sales and disposals of physical assets. Depending on the governmental organization, controls over sales and disposals of physical assets may apply to not only large or high-dollar items but also to the smallest or low-dollar items. These controls typically include the following:

- Formal declaration by the governing body as to the surplus or obsolescence of physical assets
- Making sales of surplus or obsolete physical assets available to the public
- Conducting sales of surplus or obsolete physical assets through a public auction using an independent auctioneer
- Required advertising of the public auction including date, time, and place

NOT-FOR-PROFIT ENTITIES

Unique to the consideration of fraud in financial statement audits of not-for-profit entities is the issue of *contributed physical assets*. Valuable and sometimes significant physical assets are contributed on behalf of, or for the benefit of, the not-for-profit entity or the clients it serves. Without effective controls over these types of contributions, it is possible for them to be misdirected or misappropriated. This is of special concern when a not-for-profit entity has a number of locations or affiliates.

As with assets of governmental organizations, redirecting of assets wholly or partially acquired or constructed with federal financial assistance by not-for-profit entities may also have significant repercussions. Sometimes these physical assets may be used only for purposes specifically included in the grant agreement. Therefore, if the use of such an asset is to be redirected to another bona fide function of the not-for-profit entity, permission of the grantor may be required in advance. Without such permission, provisions of the original grant agreement may require the not-for-profit entity to return ownership and control of the asset to the granting agency. If unintentional, redirections of this type would not appear to result in a fraudulent transaction.

Misappropriation of Assets Common Fraud Schemes Diversion of Program Benefits and Assets

GENERAL ISSUES AND CONCERNS

Assistance programs funded by or offered through governmental or not-for-profit entities offer very valuable benefits or assets to qualified beneficiaries. As such, they are highly susceptible to fraud, waste, and abuse. When fraud occurs through the diversion of these program benefits or assets, the governmental or not-for-profit entity is definitely harmed. More important, however, is the harm caused to the intended beneficiaries of the program.

Government and not-for-profit entities are involved in a number of programs designed to benefit thousands of individuals. In many cases, federal funds are used to operate in total or in part numerous programs offered through governmental and not-for-profit entities. Some programs typical of those provided by many government and not-for-profit entities include the following:

- Unemployment benefits
- Food stamps
- Housing assistance (ownership, renters)
- Financial aid for students
- Health care
- Job training
- Legal assistance
- Child care

In most cases, these monies are awarded as grants and the grant contract includes onerous compliance requirements. Lack of compliance with the grant provisions may result in the recipient governmental or not-for-profit entity having to repay the funds to the grantor. Therefore, an integral part of financial statement audits of governmental and not-for-profit entities relates to grant compliance requirements.

When federal funds are not spent in accordance with grant provisions, monies received under the grant become contingent liabilities of the recipient organization. As such, compliance testing is significant to not only the federal financial assistance financial statements but the basic financial statements as well.

Potential fraud risk factors related to benefit programs sponsored by or offered through governmental and not-for-profit entities include the following:

- Pressure from *constituent or special interest groups*
- Potential for programs to *generate net revenues*
- Pressure to "*use or lose*" budgeted amounts or grant awards
- Physical access to program benefits or assets, including
  - *Highly marketable or easily convertible* assets (such as supplies, food stamps, and vouchers); and
  - The ability to draw down cash using *letters of credit*

- *Decentralized* outreach, intake, and/ or eligibility certification processes
- *Self-monitoring* responsibilities due to delegation of such from funding agencies
- Complex *funding and reimbursement arrangements or restrictions,* including

- compliance and eligibility rules based on household size, income, and the like;
- Use of third parties in determining or dispensing benefits; and
- Administrative cost allowability, cost sharing, and matching

▪ Insufficient resources available for or devoted to monitoring and oversight of sub-recipients

Common Indicators of Diversion of Program Benefits and Assets

* Copies of or missing application forms and underlying supporting documentation

* Participant files lack required information (interview sheets, tax returns, and the like)

* Decentralized intake centers or centralized intake centers with little or no monitoring by management or supervisory personnel

* Inadequately trained or supervised program personnel

* Inadequate or ineffective controls over program assets

* Lack of periodic physical inventories of program assets

GOVERNMENTAL ORGANIZATIONS

Concerns in the audits of financial statements of governmental organizations associated with diversion of program benefits or assets relate primarily to personnel. As discussed previously, employees of governmental organizations are often paid less than market wages. This often results in hiring individuals who do not possess the requisite knowledge, skills, and abilities to effectively perform their assigned tasks. It may also create an *incentive* or provide the *rationalization* for the misappropriation of program benefits or assets. The *opportunity* to commit fraud with respect to program benefits and assets is often present due to too few or inadequately trained individuals in administrative or accounting or finance positions.

When the *incentive and rationalization* to commit fraud with respect to program benefits or assets is coupled with the opportunity for such, fraud may in all likelihood occur. However, in many governmental organizations, employees are subject to prosecution to the full extent of the law if caught performing illegal activities. Obviously the misappropriation of program benefits and assets could be construed as an illegal activity. Therefore, the threat of prosecution may serve as a compensating control in that it might deter someone from committing program fraud, waste, or abuse.

Often employees in small or medium-sized governmental organizations will have other responsibilities in addition to those required of them by the grant program. As such, these employees might be more likely to commit fraud with respect to program benefits or assets as they feel *pressured* to meet unrealistic performance expectations related to all assigned responsibilities. On the other hand, in large governmental organizations, sufficient resources may exist to allow employees to work full time solely within the grant program. This situation may or may not eliminate the potential pressure related to performance expectations.

NOT-FOR-PROFIT ENTITIES

Like governmental organizations, concerns in the audits of financial statements of not-for-profit entities also relate to the diversion of program benefits or assets due to personnel. Employees of not-for-profit entities are also often paid less than market wages. As a result, individuals who do not possess the requisite knowledge, skills, and abilities to effectively perform their assigned tasks are hired in grant programs. This may create an *incentive* or provide the *rationalization* for the misappropriation of program benefits or assets. The *opportunity* to commit fraud with respect to program benefits and assets is often present due to too few or inadequately trained individuals in administrative or accounting or finance positions.

Unlike governmental organizations, employees of not-for-profit entities may not be subject to prosecution to the full extent of the law if they are caught performing illegal activities. Therefore, the threat of prosecution that may serve as a compensating control in governmental organizations may not exist in not-for-profit entities.

Like their governmental counterparts, employees in small or medium-sized not-for-profit entities may have other responsibilities in addition to those required of them by a grant program. As such, these employees might be more likely to commit fraud with respect to program benefits or assets as they feel *pressured* to meet unrealistic performance expectations related to all assigned responsibilities. In large not-for-profit entities, sufficient resources may exist to allow employees to work full time solely within the grant program. This situation may or may not eliminate the potential pressure related to performance expectations.

Summary

This chapter focused on fraud schemes commonly found in governmental and not-for-profit entities. The chapter discussed in detail a number of fraudulent financial reporting as well as misappropriation of assets fraud schemes. A number of indicators were included in this chapter related to various specific fraud schemes related to both fraudulent financial reporting and misappropriation of assets. In addition, this chapter discussed a number of procedures the auditor might consider in audits of governmental or not-for-profit entities.

Practice Questions

1. What are the two most common schemes to perpetrate fraudulent financial reporting?

2. List three indicators of possible fraudulent financial reporting due to revenue recognition.

3. List three areas where improper revenue recognition may occur in governmental organizations.

4. List three areas where improper revenue recognition may occur in not-for-profit entities.

5. List three types of physical assets that are easily misappropriated from governmental and not-for-profit entities.

6. List all of the common misappropriation of assets fraud schemes discussed in this chapter.

7. List three indicators of possible misappropriation of assets due to procurement and contracting fraud.

8. List three indicators of possible misappropriation of cash receipts and disbursements.

9. List two indicators of possible misappropriation of assets due to personnel fraud.

10. List five types of program benefits that are typically subject to misappropriation.

EXEMPT ORGANIZATIONS GLOSSARY

GOVERNMENTAL TERMINOLOGY

Accounting System – The methods and records established to identify, assemble, analyze, classify, record, and report a government's transactions and to maintain accountability for the related assets and liabilities.

Accrual Basis of Accounting – The recording of financial effects on a government of transactions and other events and circumstances that have consequences for the government in the periods in which those transactions, events, and circumstances occur, rather than only in the periods in which cash is received or paid by the government.

Ad Valorem Tax – A tax based on value (such as a property tax).

Advance From Other Funds – An asset account used to record noncurrent portions of a long-term debt owed by one fund to another fund within the same reporting entity. (See **Due to Other Funds** and *Interfund Receivable/ Payable*).

Agency Funds – A fund normally used to account for assets held by a government as an agent for individuals, private organizations or other governments and/ or other funds.

Appropriation – A legal authorization granted by a legislative body to make expenditures and to incur obligations for specific purposes. An appropriation is usually limited in amount and time it may be expended.

Assigned Fund Balance – A portion of fund balance that includes amounts that are constrained by the government's intent to be used for specific purposes, but that are neither restricted nor committed.

Basis of Accounting – A term used to refer to *when* revenues, expenditures, expenses, and transfers, and related assets and liabilities are recognized in the accounts and reported in the financial statements. Specifically, it relates to the timing of the measurements made, regardless of the nature of the measurement. (See **Accrual Basis of Accounting, Cash Basis of Accounting,** and **Modified Accrual Basis of Accounting**).

Bond – A written promise to pay a specified sum of money (the face value or principal amount) at a specified date or dates in the future (the maturity dates[s]), together with periodic interest at a specified rate. Sometimes, however, all or a substantial part of the interest is included in the face value of the security. The difference between a note and bond is that the latter is issued for a longer period and requires greater legal formality.

Business Type Activities – Those activities of a government carried out primarily to provide specific services in exchange for a specific user charge.

Capital Grants – Grants restricted by the grantor for the acquisition and/ or construction of (a) capital asset(s).

Capital Projects Fund – A fund used to account for and report financial resources that are restricted, committed, or assigned to expenditures for capital outlays, including the acquisition or construction of capital facilities and other capital assets. Capital project funds exclude those types of capital-related outflows financed by proprietary funds or for assets that will be held in trust for individuals, private organizations, or other governments.

Cash Basis of Accounting – A basis of accounting that requires the recognition of transactions only when cash is received or disbursed.

Committed Fund Balance – A portion of fund balance that includes amounts that can only be used for specific purposes pursuant to constraints imposed by formal action of the government's highest level of decision-making authority.

Consumption Method – The method of accounting that requires the recognition of an expenditure/ expense as inventories are used.

Contributed Capital – Contributed capital is created when a general capital asset is *transferred* to a proprietary fund or when a grant is received that is externally restricted to capital acquisition or construction. Contributions restricted to capital acquisition and construction and capital assets received from developers are reported in the operating statement as a separate item after nonoperating revenues and expenses.

Debt Service Fund – A fund used to account for and report financial resources that are restricted, committed, or assigned to expenditure for principal and interest. Debt service funds should be used to report resources if legally mandated. Financial resources that are being accumulated for principal and interest maturing in future years should also be reported debt service funds.

Deferred Revenue – Amounts for which asset recognition criteria (receivable) have been met, but for which revenue recognition criteria have not been met. Under the modified accrual basis of accounting, amounts that are measurable but not available are classified as deferred revenue. Cash received in advance of the period of applicability is also recorded as deferred revenue.

Deficit – (a) The excess of the liabilities of a fund over its assets. (b) The excess of expenditures over revenues during an accounting period, or in the case of proprietary funds, the excess of expenses over revenues during an accounting period.

Disbursement – A payment made in cash or by check. Expenses are only recognized at the time physical cash is disbursed.

Due From Other Funds – A current asset account used to indicate account reflecting amounts owed to a particular fund by another fund for goods sold or services rendered. This account includes only short-term obligations on open account, not interfund loans.

Due to Other Funds – A current liability account reflecting amounts owed by a particular fund to another fund for goods sold or services rendered. This account includes only short-term obligations on an open account, not interfund loans.

Fund Financial Statements – Each fund has its own set of self-balancing accounts and fund financial statements that focus on information about the government's governmental, proprietary, and fiduciary fund types.

Enabling Legislation – Legislation that authorizes a government to assess, levy, charge, or otherwise mandate payment of resources from external resource providers, and includes a legally enforceable requirement that those resources be used for the specific purposes stipulated in the legislation.

Encumbrances – Commitments related to unperformed (executory) contracts for goods or services. Used in budgeting, encumbrances are *not* GAAP expenditures or liabilities, but represent the estimated amount of expenditures ultimately to result if unperformed contracts in process are completed.

Enterprise Fund – A fund established to account for operations financed and operated in a manner similar to private business enterprises (such as gas, utilities, transit systems, and parking garages). Usually, the governing body intends that costs of providing goods or services to the general public be recovered primarily through user charges.

Expenditures – Decreases in net financial resources. Expenditures include current operating expenses requiring the present or future use of net current assets, debt service and capital outlays, intergovernmental grants, entitlements, and shared revenues.

Expenses – Outflows or other using up of assets or incurrences of liabilities, or a combination of both, from delivering or producing goods, rendering services, or carrying out other activities that constitute the entity's ongoing major or central operations.

Fund – A fiscal and accounting entity with a self-balancing set of accounts in which cash and other financial resources, all related liabilities and residual equities, or balances, and changes therein, are recorded and segregated to carry on specific activities or attain certain objectives in accordance with special regulations, restrictions, or limitations.

Fund Balance – The difference between fund assets and fund liabilities of the generic fund types within the governmental category of funds.

Fund Type – The 11 generic funds that all transactions of a government are recorded into. The 11 fund types are as follows: general, special revenue, debt service, capital projects, permanent, enterprise, internal service, private purpose trust, pension trust, investment trust, and agency.

GASB – The Governmental Accounting Standards Board (GASB) was organized in 1984 by the Financial Accounting Foundation (FAF) to establish standards of financial accounting and reporting for state and local governmental entities. Its standards guide the preparation of external financial reports of those entities.

General Fund – The fund within the governmental category used to account for all financial resources except those required to be accounted for in another governmental fund.

General-Purpose Governments – General-purpose governments are governmental entities that provide a range of services, such as states, cities, counties, towns, and villages.

Governmental Funds – Funds used to account for the acquisition, use, and balances of spendable financial resources and the related current liabilities, except those accounted for in proprietary funds and fiduciary funds. Essentially, these funds are accounting segregations of financial resources. Spendable assets are assigned to a particular government fund type according to the purposes for which they may or must be used. Current liabilities are assigned to the fund type from which they are to be paid. The difference between the assets and liabilities of governmental fund types is referred to as fund balance. The measurement focus in these funds types is on the determination of financial position and changes in financial position (sources, uses, and balances of financial resources) rather than on net income determination.

Government-Wide Financial Statements – The government-wide financial statements are highly aggregated financial statements that present financial information for all assets (including infrastructure capital assets), liabilities, and net assets of a primary government and its component units, except for fiduciary funds. The government-wide financial statements use the economic resources measurement focus and accrual basis of accounting.

Infrastructure Assets – Infrastructure assets are long-lived capital assets that normally are stationary in nature and normally can be preserved for a significantly greater number of years than most capital assets. Examples of infrastructure assets are roads, bridges, tunnels, drainage systems, water and sewer systems, dams, and lighting systems. Buildings, except those that are an ancillary part of a network of infrastructure assets, are not considered infrastructure assets.

Internal Service Fund – A generic fund type within the proprietary category used to account for the financing of goods or services provided by one department or agency to other departments or agencies of a government, or to other governments, on a cost-reimbursement basis.

Investment Trust Fund – A generic fund type within the fiduciary category used by a government in a fiduciary capacity, such as to maintain its cash and investment pool for other governments.

Major Funds – A government's general fund (or its equivalent), other individual governmental type, and enterprise funds that meet specific quantitative criteria, and any other governmental or enterprise fund that a government's officials believe is particularly important to financial statement users.

Management's Discussion and Analysis (MD&A) – MD&A is RSI that introduces the basic financial statements by presenting certain financial information as well as management's analytical insights on that information.

Measurement Focus – The accounting convention that determines (a) which assets and which liabilities are included on a government's balance sheet and where they are reported, and (b) whether an operating statement presents information on the flow of financial resources (revenues and expenditures) or information on the flow of economic resources (revenues and expenses).

Modified Accrual Basis of Accounting – The basis of accounting adapted to the governmental fund type measurement focus. Revenues and other financial resource increments are recognized when they become both *measurable* and *available to finance expenditures of the current period. Available* means collectible in the current period or soon enough thereafter to be used to pay liabilities of the current period. Expenditures are recognized when the fund liability is incurred and expected to be paid from current resources except for (a) inventories of materials and supplies that may be considered expenditures either when purchased or when used, and (b) prepaid insurance and similar items that may be considered expenditures either when paid for or when consumed. All governmental funds are accounted for using the modified accrual basis of accounting in fund financial statements.

Modified Approach – Rules that allow infrastructure assets that are part of a network or subsystem of a network not to be depreciated as long as certain requirements are met.

Nonspendable Fund Balance – The portion of fund valance that includes amounts that cannot be spent because they are either (a) not in spendable form, or (b) legally or contractually required to be maintained intact.

Pension Trust Fund – A trust fund used to account for a PERS. Pension trust funds use the accrual basis of accounting and the flow of economic resources measurement focus.

Permanent Fund – A generic fund type under the governmental category used to report resources that are legally restricted to the extent that only earnings, and not principal, may be used for purposes that support the reporting government's programs and, therefore, are for the benefit of the government or its citizenry. (Permanent funds do not include private-purpose trust funds, which should be used when the government is required to use the principal or earnings for the benefit of individuals, private organizations, or other governments).

Private Purpose Trust Fund – A general fund type under the fiduciary category used to report resources held and administered by the reporting government acting in a fiduciary capacity for individuals, other governments, or private organizations.

Proprietary Funds – The government category used to account for a government's ongoing organizations and activities that are similar to those often found in the private sector (these are enterprise and internal service funds). All assets, liabilities, equities, revenues, expenses, and transfers relating to the government's business and quasi-business activities are accounted for through proprietary funds. Proprietary funds should apply all applicable GASB pronouncements and those GAAP applicable to similar businesses in the private sector, unless those conflict with GASB pronouncements. These funds use the accrual basis of accounting in conjunction with the flow of economic resources measurement focus.

Purchases Method – The method under which inventories are recorded as expenditures when acquired.

Restricted Fund Balance – Portion of fund valance that reflects constraints placed on the use of resources (other than nonspendable items) that are either (a) externally imposed by creditor such as through debt covenants, grantors, contributors, or laws or regulations of other governments, or (b) imposed by law through constitutional provisions or enabling legislation.

Required Supplementary Information (RSI) – GAAP specify that certain information be presented as RSI.

Special-Purpose Governments – Special-purpose governments are legally separate entities that perform only one activity or only a few activities, such as cemetery districts, school districts, colleges and universities, utilities, hospitals and other health care organizations, and public employee retirement systems.

Special Revenue Fund – A fund that *must* have revenue or proceeds from specific revenue sources which are either restricted or committed for a specific purpose other than debt service or capital projects. This definition means that in order to be considered a special revenue fund, there must be one or more revenue sources upon which reporting the activity in a separate fund is predicated.

Transfers – All interfund transfers, such as legally authorized transfers from a fund receiving revenue to a fund through which the resources are to be expended, where there is no intent to repay. Interfund transfers are recorded on the operating statement.

Unassigned Fund Balance – Residual classification for the general fund. This classification represents fund balance that has not been assigned to other funds and that has not been restricted, committed, or assigned to specific purposes within the general fund. The general fund should be the only fund that reports a positive unassigned fund valance amount. In other funds, if expenditures incurred for specific purposes exceeded the amounts restricted, committed, or assigned to those purposes,

Unrestricted Fund Balance – The total of committed fund balance, assigned fund balance, and unassigned fund balance.

NOT-FOR-PROFIT TERMINOLOGY

Charitable Lead Trust – A trust established in connection with a split-interest agreement, in which the not-for-profit organization receives distributions during the agreement's term. Upon termination of the trust, the remainder of the trust assets is paid to the donor or to third-party beneficiaries designated by the donor.

Charitable Remainder Trust – A trust established in connection with a split-interest agreement, in which the donor or a third-party beneficiary receives specified distributions during the agreement's term. Upon termination of the trust, a not-for-profit organization receives the assets remaining in the trust.

Collections – Works of art, historical treasures, or similar assets that are (a) held for public exhibition, education, or research in furtherance of public service rather than financial gain, (b) protected, kept unencumbered, cared for, and preserved, and (c) subject to an organizational policy that requires the proceeds of items that are sold to be used to acquire other items for collections.

Conditional Promise to Give – A promise to give that depends on the occurrence of a specified future and uncertain event to bind the promisor.

Contribution – An unconditional transfer of cash or other assets to an entity or a settlement or cancellation of its liabilities in a voluntary nonreciprocal transfer by another entity acting other than as an owner.

Costs of Joint Activities – Costs of joint activities are costs incurred for a joint activity. Costs of joint activities may include joint costs and costs other than joint costs. Costs other than joint costs are costs that are identifiable with a particular function, such as program, fundraising, management and general, and membership development costs.

Donor-Imposed Restriction – A donor stipulation that specifies a use for the contributed asset that is more specific than broad limits resulting from the nature of the organization, the environment in which it operates, and the purposes specified in its articles of incorporation or bylaws, or comparable documents for an unincorporated association. A restriction on an organization's use of the asset contributed may be temporary or permanent.

Functional Classification – A method of grouping expenses according to the purpose for which the costs are incurred. The primary functional classifications are program services and supporting activities.

Joint Activity – A joint activity is an activity that is part of the fundraising function and has elements of one or more other functions, such as programs, management and general, membership development, or any other functional category used by the entity.

Joint Costs – Joint costs are the costs of conducting joint activities that are not identifiable with a particular component of the activity.

Natural Expense Classification – A method of grouping expenses according to the kinds of economic benefits received in incurring those expenses. Examples of natural expense classifications include salaries and wages, employee benefits, supplies, rent, and utilities.

Permanently Restricted Net Assets – The part of the net assets of a not-for-profit organization resulting (a) from contributions and other inflows of assets whose use by the organization is limited by donor-imposed stipulations that neither expire by passage of time nor can be fulfilled or otherwise removed by actions of the organization, (b) from other asset enhancements and diminishments subject to the same kinds of stipulations, and (c) from reclassifications from (or to) other classes of net assets as a consequence of donor-imposed stipulations.

Promise to Give – A written or oral agreement to contribute cash or other assets to another entity. A promise to give may be either conditional or unconditional.

Temporarily Restricted Net Assets – The part of the net assets of a not-for-profit organization resulting (a) from contributions and other inflows of assets whose use by the organization is limited by donor-imposed stipulations that either expire by the passage of time or can be fulfilled and removed by actions of the organization pursuant to those stipulations, (b) from other asset enhancements and diminishments subject to the same kinds of stipulations, and (c) from reclassifications to (or from) other classes of net assets as a consequence of donor-imposed stipulations, their expiration by passage of time, or their fulfillment and removal by actions of the organization pursuant to those stipulations.

Unrestricted Net Assets – The part of net assets of a not-for-profit organization that is neither permanently restricted nor temporarily restricted by donor-imposed stipulations.

SINGLE AUDIT & YELLOW BOOK TERMINOLOGY

Attestation Engagements – Attestation engagements concern examining, reviewing, or performing agreed-upon procedures on a subject matter or an assertion about a subject matter and reporting on the results.

Compliance Supplement – A document issued annually in the Spring by the OMB to provide guidance to auditors.

Data Collection Form – A form submitted to the Federal Audit Clearinghouse which provides information about the auditor, the auditee and its federal programs, and the results of the audit.

Federal Financial Assistance – Assistance that non-federal entities receive or administer in the form of grants, loans, loan guarantees, property, cooperative agreements, interest subsidies, insurance, food commodities, direct appropriations, or other assistance, but does not include amounts received as reimbursement for services rendered to individuals in accordance with guidance issued by the Director.

Financial Audits – Financial audits are primarily concerned with providing reasonable assurance about whether financial statements are presented fairly, in all material respects, in conformity with generally accepted accounting principles (GAAP) or with a comprehensive basis of accounting other than GAAP.

GAGAS – Generally Accepted Government Auditing Standards issued by the GAO. They are also commonly known as the Yellow Book.

GAO – The United States Government Accountability Office. Among their responsibilities is the issuance of Generally Accepted Government Auditing Standards (a.k.a. the Yellow Book).

OMB – The Office of Management and Budget. OMB assists the President in the development and implementation of budget, program, management, and regulatory policies.

Pass-Through Entity – A non-federal entity that provides federal awards to a subrecipient to carry out a federal program.

Performance Audits – Performance audits entail an objective and systematic examination of evidence to provide an independent assessment of the performance and management of a program against objective criteria as well as assessments that provide a prospective focus or that synthesize information on best practices or cross-cutting issues.

Program-Specific Audit – An audit of one federal program.

Single Audit – An audit of a non-federal entity that includes the entity's financial statements and Federal awards.

Single Audit Guide – This AICPA Audit Guide formally titled Government Auditing Standards and Circular A-133 Audits (the Single Audit Guide) is the former Statement of Position (SOP) 98-3. The Single Audit Guide provides guidance on the auditor's responsibilities when conducting a single audit or program-specific audit in accordance with the Single Audit Act and Circular A-133.

Subrecipient – A non-federal entity that receives federal awards through another non-federal entity to carry out a federal program, but does not include an individual who receives financial assistance through such awards.

INDEX

A

AICPA 1-3, 3-1, 3-2, 3-9, 3-11, 4-13
Analytical 3-13, 5-8, 5-9, 5-16, 5-17
Audit Committee 2-3

C

Cash 1-6, 2-13, 3-5, 3-13, 4-9, 4-10, 4-12, 5-4, 5-12,
    5-15, 5-22, 5-23, 5-24, 5-28, 5-32, 5-37
Communication 1-5, 1-7, 3-15

D

Discussion 3-11, 3-12, 4-3, 5-6
Documentation 3-10, 4-2, 5-4, 5-12, 5-19, 5-22, 5-33

E

Evidence 2-4, 2-7, 3-2, 3-6, 3-9, 3-10, 3-12, 3-15, 4-16,
    5-6, 5-10, 5-29

F

Financial Statements 1-2, 3-2, 3-3, 4-8, 4-15, 5-12,
    5-16, 5-27
Fraudulent Financial Reporting 1-4, 3-2, 3-3, 3-9, 3-10,
    3-11, 3-14, 4-3, 4-10, 4-11, 4-12, 5-1, 5-2, 5-4, 5-5, 5-6,
    5-7, 5-8, 5-9, 5-10, 5-12, 5-13, 5-16, 5-18, 5-35, 5-36

I

Internal Control 3-2, 3-5, 3-10, 3-11, 3-14, 3-15, 4-4,
    4-7, 4-8, 4-9, 4-10, 5-2, 5-18, 5-29

M

Material 1-2, 3-2, 3-3, 3-4, 3-5, 3-6, 3-7, 3-9, 3-10,
    3-11, 3-12, 3-13, 3-14, 4-4, 4-7, 4-9, 4-10, 4-11, 4-12,
    5-6, 5-8, 5-9, 5-10, 5-12, 5-13, 5-14, 5-15, 5-16, 5-23,
    5-26, 5-27
Misappropriation of Assets 1-4, 3-2, 3-3, 3-10, 4-10,
    4-11, 4-12, 5-1, 5-15, 5-16, 5-18, 5-19, 5-21, 5-22, 5-23,
    5-24, 5-25, 5-26, 5-27, 5-35, 5-37
Monitoring 5-32, 5-33

O

Opportunity 3-4, 3-5, 3-15, 4-9, 4-10, 4-18, 5-22, 5-23,
    5-24, 5-33, 5-34

P

Planning 2-1, 2-4, 3-6, 3-7, 3-15, 4-4, 4-12, 4-16
Professional Skepticism 3-6, 3-7, 3-8, 3-11, 3-14, 3-16,
    3-17, 4-16

R

Rationalize 3-5, 3-6, 3-10, 4-3, 4-10, 5-12
Risk Assessment 3-11, 3-12, 3-13, 4-13
Risk Factors 3-4, 3-11, 4-4, 4-7, 5-32

T

Turnover 3-14, 4-7, 4-8, 4-13, 5-22

FRAUD RISK IN GOVERNMENTAL AND NOT-FOR-PROFIT ORGANIZATIONS

BY LYNDA DENNIS, CPA, CGFO, PH.D.

Solutions

The AICPA offers a free, daily, e-mailed newsletter covering the day's top business and financial articles as well as video content, research and analysis concerning CPAs and those who work with the accounting profession. Visit the CPA Letter Daily news box on the www.aicpa.org home page to sign up. You can opt out at any time, and only the AICPA can use your e-mail address or personal information.

Have a technical accounting or auditing question? So did 23,000 other professionals who contacted the AICPA's accounting and auditing Technical Hotline last year. The objectives of the hotline are to enhance members' knowledge and application of professional judgment by providing free, prompt, high-quality technical assistance by phone concerning issues related to: accounting principles and financial reporting; auditing, attestation, compilation and review standards. The team extends this technical assistance to representatives of governmental units. The hotline can be reached at 1-877-242-7212.

SOLUTIONS

CHAPTER 1

Solutions to Practice Questions

1. Ways to prevent, detect and deter computer fraud include the following:

    - Separation and rotation of duties both within and external to the technology function,
    - Timely update of accessible computer applications when personnel change jobs or when the requirements of their current position change,
    - Periodic and surprise inspections and security reviews,
    - all control policies and procedures required to be written (zero tolerance for deviations from this policy, and
    - Offline controls and limits such as batch controls and hash totals where indicated and cost-effective

2. Fraud research consistently indicates the common characteristics of individuals that perpetrate financial statement fraud are

    - a trusted employee
    - dedicated and often works long hours,
    - dislikes mandatory vacation policies,
    - resents cross-training,
    - seen as likeable and generous, and is
    - deceptive and usually an adept liar.

Solutions to Knowledge Check Questions

1.

    a. Incorrect. Organizational culture of arrogance and management entitlement is a general warning sign of fraud.
    b. Incorrect. Overly centralized control over financial reporting is a general warning sign of fraud.
    c. Correct. Open and honest communication between key accounting or finance personnel and top management of the organization is not a general warning sign of fraud.
    d. Incorrect. Transactions that lack economic purpose may be indicative of kickbacks as well as misappropriation of assets.

2.

    a.   Incorrect. Mandatory background checks prior to starting work are a general technique to prevent, detect, or deter personnel fraud.

    b.   Incorrect. Routine visits to offsite locations are a general technique to prevent, detect, or deter personnel fraud.

    c.   Incorrect. Printing accrued and unused leave hours on employee pay check stubs is a general technique to prevent, detect, or deter personnel fraud.

    d.   Correct. Though a lack of performance feedback mechanisms is considered a personal factor to encourage computer fraud, the materials do not indicate this as a general technique to prevent, detect, or deter personnel fraud.

CHAPTER 2

Solutions to Practice Questions

1.   The major characteristics are that governmental organizations

- are public organizations,
- provide goods and services to the general public using funds typically secured from involuntary resource providers,
- make decisions in a political environment, and
- provide goods and services without regard to a profit motive.

2.   The major differentiating characteristics are that

- not-for-profit entities receive significant contributions of resources from donors not expecting commensurate or proportionate financial return,
- not-for-profit entities operate for purposes other than to provide goods or services at a profit, and
- ownership interests are absent.

3.   The primary users include

- citizens,
- legislative and oversight bodies, and
- investors and creditors.

4.   The primary users are

- resource providers,
- constituents, and
- governing and oversight bodies.

Solutions to Knowledge Check Questions

1.

    a.   Correct. A unique characteristic of governmental organizations is that they are public organizations.

    b.   Incorrect. A unique characteristic of governmental organizations is that they provide goods and services to the general public using funds typically secured from involuntary resource providers.

    c.   Incorrect. A requirement to conduct business in a public forum is often a significant impediment to timely responses to sensitive issues.

    d.   Incorrect. Governments may or may not be required to recover the full cost of providing some or all services through user fees.

2.

    a.   Incorrect. Contributions received by a not-for-profit entity may be subject to donor restrictions imposing time or use restrictions either on a temporary or permanent basis.

    b.   Correct. In order to fund goods or services provided to the community for little or no cost, not-for-profit entities have traditionally relied on contributions from individuals and businesses.

    c.   Incorrect. Contributions received by a not-for-profit entity may be subject to temporary donor restrictions.

    d.   Incorrect. Grant provisions often require a significant amount of control over and accountability for funds disbursed to not-for-profit entities.

3.

    a.   Correct. Not-for-profit entities often receive contributions in the form of grants from governmental agencies or other not-for-profit entities.

    b.   Incorrect. Contributions received by a not-for-profit entity may be subject to permanent donor restrictions.

    c.   Incorrect. Not-for-profit entities are organized for and operated to achieve a particular mission rather than to make a profit from their operations.

    d.   Incorrect. Not-for-profit entities do not have stockholders.

4.

    a.   Correct. Governmental financial reports are used in decision-making and in assessing accountability.

    b.   Incorrect. Public accountability does not ignore that taxpayers are entitled to know what their government is doing and how.

    c.   Incorrect. The objectives of external financial reporting by state and local governments do include the obligation to be publicly accountable.

    d.   Incorrect. As defined by GASB, the primary users of external governmental financial reports include citizens and investors (creditors) in addition to legislative and oversight bodies.

CHAPTER 3

Solutions to Practice Questions

1. The two additional areas are

    - improper revenue recognition and
    - risk of management override.

2. For those auditors with long-term or close relationships with their governmental or not-for-profit clients, it may prove difficult to adopt the required level of professional skepticism. Even when auditors feel they have assumed the level of professional skepticism required by AU-C section 316, the "appearance" of professional skepticism may not be apparent to those outside the audit firm.

    Long-term auditor-client relationships or multiyear assignment of professional staff to a particular audit entity may give the auditor a false sense of security with respect to the organization under audit. In these situations (whether or not a long-term relationship exists between the auditor and the organization), engagement or firm staff may believe client personnel to be honest and to act with integrity. Because it may be difficult for audit staff members to exercise appropriate professional skepticism in these circumstances, the engagement team should constantly strive to put aside past relationships with the organization.

Solutions to Knowledge Check Questions

1.

    a. Incorrect. AU-C section 240 does not limit financial statement fraud to fraudulent financial reporting.
    b. Incorrect. AU-C section 240 does not limit financial statement fraud to misappropriation of assets.
    c. Correct. AU-C section 240 defines financial statement fraud as fraudulent financial reporting and misappropriation of assets.
    d. Incorrect. AU-C section 240 identifies management and those charged with governance as having responsibility for the prevention and detection of fraud.

2.

    a. Correct. AU-C section 200 requires the auditor to exercise professional skepticism in all audits.
    b. Incorrect. AU-C section 200 requires the auditor to exercise professional skepticism in areas other than those relating to fraud.
    c. Incorrect. AU-C section 200 requires the auditor to exercise professional skepticism in all years, not just a first-year audit.
    d. Incorrect. AU-C section 200 requires all members of the audit engagement team to exercise professional skepticism.

3.

    a.   Incorrect. An objective of AU-C section 240 is to identify and assess the risks of material misstatement due to fraud.

    b.   Incorrect. This is not an objective of AU-C section 240.

    c.   Correct. This is an objective of AU-C section 240.

    d.   Incorrect. AU-C section 240 requires the auditor to respond appropriately to fraud or suspected fraud identified during the audit.

4.

    a.   Incorrect. Obtaining an understanding is specific risk assessment procedure required under AU-C section 240.

    b.   Incorrect. Discussing fraud risks is a specific risk assessment procedure required under AU-C section 240.

    c.   Correct. This is not a specific risk assessment procedure required under AU-C section 240.

    d.   Incorrect. Evaluating whether identified unusual or unexpected relationships indicate risk of material misstatement is a specific risk assessment procedure required under AU-C section 240.

CHAPTER 4

Solutions to Practice Questions

1.   The three steps are as follows:

- The fraud is *committed.*
- Perpetrators *receive the benefits* of the fraud.
- The fraud is *concealed.*

2.   Employees of governmental organizations are under constant *pressure* to provide more and higher-quality services with fewer resources. When the economy is in decline, there is added pressure on governmental organizations to maintain current tax rates and user charges. This places pressure on the management of governmental organizations to meet or improve upon budgeted amounts. An *incentive* to overstate revenues or to understate expenses/ expenditures may be created by this pressure.

3.   The lack of personnel or the lack of sufficiently qualified personnel is prevalent in administrative, and accounting and finance functions in governmental organizations. The resulting lack of, or ineffective, internal controls creates *opportunities* for fraud.

Governmental organizations often have a number of locations taking cash in payment of services such as recreation centers, police departments, libraries, and the like. Lacking or ineffective controls create *opportunities* for fraud in these areas also. It is highly likely the amounts of many of these revenues are not material to the financial statements of the governmental organization taken as a whole. However, one of the objectives of financial reporting for governmental organizations is public accountability. Situations such as these, while not material to the financial statements, are material to public accountability.

4. Because of the large number of grants or other intergovernmental revenues common to most governmental organizations, *revenue recognition* may be of particular concern to the auditor with respect to the consideration of fraud. The concern here is more with misstatements due to fraudulent financial reporting than misappropriation of assets. Generally accepted accounting principles related to recording exchange and non-exchange transactions contribute to the issue of proper revenue recognition in governmental organizations.

    However, it is possible that in some governments, revenue recognition may not be a fraud risk area from the perspective of misappropriation of assets. In some localities, all material revenues are received via electronic funds transfers or checks on a periodic basis from another governmental agency. This holds true for municipal property taxes in a number of states where the county acts as the tax assessor and collector for all taxing authorities within its jurisdiction. For many governments, revenues received in cash or at offsite locations with few internal controls are often immaterial to the financial statements taken as a whole.

5. Examples include

    - allowances for material uncollectible receivables such as pledges, special assessments, dues, and customer receivables;
    - split-interest agreements;
    - estimated useful lives of capital assets;
    - estimates of accrued compensated absences;
    - estimated contingent liabilities for litigation, claims, and assessments;
    - allocation of joint costs; and
    - functional allocations of expenses.

Solutions to Knowledge Check Questions

1.

a. Correct. Governmental organizations may sometimes intentionally misstate functional expenses. It is incorrect to assume governments would never intentionally misstate functional expenses.
b. Incorrect. Governmental organizations may intentionally misstate functional expenses to circumvent legal requirements.
c. Incorrect. Governmental organizations may intentionally misstate functional expenses to comply with bond covenants.
d. Incorrect. GASB Statement No. 34, as amended, does require the reporting of expenses at the government-wide level by functional classification in the statement of activities.

2.

a. Correct. This is a unique area that may be a target for potential fraud.
b. Incorrect. This is an area that may be a target for potential fraud, but is not unique to not-for-profit entities.
c. Incorrect. Not-for-profit entities do not have owners with a profit motive.
d. Incorrect. This is an area that may be a target for potential fraud, but is not unique to not-for-profit entities.

3.

   a. Correct. Employees of not-for-profit entities are often paid less than their counterparts in the private sector.
   b. Incorrect. Employees of not-for-profit entities may feel pressured to appear efficient or effective in order to attract donors or to obtain grant funds.
   c. Incorrect. Not-for-profit entities may have very high turnover in accounting and other support positions.
   d. Incorrect. Not-for-profit entities do not have owners. Those charged with governance may pressure employees to do more with less, however.

4.

   a. Incorrect. The accounting estimates made by governmental organizations do include allowances for material uncollectible receivables such as taxes, special assessments, and customer receivables.
   b. Incorrect. The accounting estimates made by governmental organizations do include functional allocations of direct and indirect costs.
   c. Correct. The accounting estimates made by governmental organizations include estimated useful lives of capital assets.
   d. Incorrect. Accounting estimates made by government engineers relating to the condition of infrastructure assets accounted for using the modified approach are subject to management override the same as other estimates.

CHAPTER 5

Solutions to Practice Questions

1. The most common financial reporting fraud schemes are

    - premature revenue recognition, and
    - premature expense/ expenditure recognition.

2. Indicators of possible fraudulent financial reporting due to revenue recognition are

    - overstatement of earnings/ increases in net assets or net position,
    - fictitious revenues,
    - improper application of revenue recognition principles,
    - overstatement of assets, and
    - understatement of allowances for receivables.

3. Areas where improper revenue recognition may occur in governmental organizations include

    - nonexchange transactions,
    - grant revenues,
    - revenues of governmental activities, and
    - pledged revenues.

4. Areas where improper revenue recognition may occur in not-for-profit entities include

   - contributions,
   - membership dues,
   - fundraising,
   - split-interest agreements,
   - grants, and
   - healthcare receivables.

5. Types of physical assets that are easily misappropriated from governmental and not-for-profit entities include the following:

   - Cash
   - Cash equivalents, such as food stamps, tuition vouchers, and lottery tickets, either processed or kept as inventory
   - Legally confiscated items
   - Inventories of supplies, etc., and physical assets that are
     - Small in size,
     - High in value,
     - High in consumer demand,
     - Easily convertible to cash, and
     - Lacking in ownership identification

   - Equipment that is subject to personal or non-program use, such as cellular phones, digital cameras, computers, vehicles, and tools
   - Physical assets susceptible to personal use or redirection, such as unused or out-of-the-way buildings, vacant land, obsolete equipment, and abandoned assets

6. Common misappropriation of assets fraud schemes discussed in this chapter are

   - embezzlement of cash receipts and fraudulent disbursements,
   - personnel fraud,
   - diversion of physical assets,
   - procurement and contracting fraud, and
   - diversion of program benefits and assets.

7. Common indicators of the potential for the misappropriation of assets due to procurement or contracting fraud include the following:

   - Unusual vendor names and addresses
   - Copies of invoices, purchase orders, or receiving documents rather than original documentation
   - Orders for materials and supplies already on hand in sufficient quantities or that are scheduled for disposal or discontinued use due to obsolescence
   - Orders for materials and supplies not consistent with the operations or mission of the government or not-for-profit entity
   - Delivery addresses different than the purchaser's physical locations
   - Purchases falling just below the threshold for required next-level approval (in quantity or amount)
   - Split purchases using purchase orders, vendor invoices, change orders, and the like
   - Payments to vendors not on approved vendor lists
   - Signature of management or supervisory personnel on documents typically signed by subordinate personnel

- Suppliers or contractors receiving significant amounts of business from the organization
- Prices in excess of market or expected market especially when large quantities are ordered
- Complaints from vendors or suppliers regarding not being allowed to bid, stringent bid specifications or procedures, or inadequate time allowed for responding to bid requests
- Contract award patterns that may indicate bids are being rotated
- Low quality combined with high prices including high product failure or return rates
- Sole source procurements in significant number or without adequate justification

8. Indicators of possible misappropriation of cash receipts and disbursements include the following:

- Missing or out-of-sequence blank checks
- Significant bank reconciling items without reasonable explanation
- Second payee or unusual endorsements on checks
- Missing cancelled checks
- Unusual disbursement transactions or transactions lacking sufficient supporting documentation.
- Citizen or customer complaints about amounts they owe the organization (for taxes, services rendered, contribution pledges, and the like)

9. Common indicators of the potential for the misappropriation of assets due to personnel fraud include the following:

- Unusual or second-party endorsements on payroll checks
- Employees without the usual withholdings related to employer provided or offered benefits (insurance, retirement, savings bonds, and the like)
- Missing, unusual-looking, or altered time and attendance records in general or frequently for the same employee(s)
- Time and attendance records signed by someone other than the usual supervisor in general or frequently for the same employee(s)

10. Types of program benefits that are typically subject to misappropriation include

- unemployment benefits;
- food stamps;
- housing assistance (ownership, renters);
- financial aid for students;
- health care;
- job training;
- legal assistance; and
- childcare.

Solutions to Knowledge Check Questions

1.

a. Correct. Exchange transactions are not an area of concern; however, nonexchange transactions are an area of concern.
b. Incorrect. Grant revenues are an area of concern.
c. Incorrect. Pledged revenues are an area of concern.
d. Incorrect. Activities of governmental activities are a concern as they are required to be reported as program or general revenues in the statement of activities.

2.

    a.   Incorrect. Fund raising is an area of concern.

    b.   Correct. Charges for services are not an area of concern.

    c.   Incorrect. Grants are an area of concern as they may represent exchange transactions, contributions, or both.

    d.   Incorrect. Membership dues are an area of concern as they may represent exchange transactions, contributions, or both.

3.

    a.   Incorrect. Ascertain if any significant budget adjustments were made at, near, or after year-end is an appropriate analytical procedure.

    b.   Incorrect. Review significant transfers between classes of net assets or net position made at, near, or after year-end is an appropriate analytical procedure.

    c.   Correct. Comparing gains and losses on sales of capital assets for the current year to the prior year is not an appropriate analytical procedure.

    d.   Incorrect. Comparing volume of *purchases by vendor for significant increases* to the prior year is an appropriate analytical procedure.

4.

    a.   Incorrect. An opportunity for the misappropriation of assets does exist in governmental and not-for-profit entities whenever cash is collected at or disbursed from a number of locations.

    b.   Correct. In consideration of fraud with respect to cash receipts and disbursements, the effectiveness of controls over disbursement transactions initiated at offsite locations is a concern.

    c.   Incorrect. The consideration of fraud with respect to cash receipts and disbursements related to missing or ineffective controls is a concern.

    d.   Incorrect. Limited administrative and/ or finance and accounting personnel in governmental and not-for-profit entities is often a concern associated with the consideration of fraud with respect to cash receipts and disbursements.

5.

    a.   Correct. Such assets may typically be used in the edification or enhancement of specific or any law enforcement activities.

    b.   Incorrect. All or some confiscated assets may revert to the state in which they were confiscated.

    c.   Incorrect. Assets confiscated often represent the types of assets that are subject to misappropriation.

    d.   Incorrect. Misappropriation of assets confiscated in law enforcement activities is often newsworthy.

Learn More

AICPA CPE

Thank you for selecting AICPA as your continuing professional education provider. We have a diverse offering of CPE courses to help you expand your skillset and develop your competencies. Choose from hundreds of different titles spanning the major subject matter areas relevant to CPAs and CGMAs, including:

- Governmental & Not-for-Profit accounting, auditing, and updates
- Internal control and fraud
- Audits of Employee Benefit Plans and 401(k) plans
- Individual and corporate tax updates
- A vast array of courses in other areas of accounting & auditing, controllership, management, consulting, taxation, and more!

Get your CPE when and where you want

- Self-study training options that includes on-demand, webcasts, and text formats with superior quality and a broad portfolio of topics, including bundled products like –
  - ➤ CPExpress for immediate access to hundreds of one and two-credit hour online courses for just-in-time learning at a price that is right
  - ➤ Annual Webcast Pass offering live Q&A with experts and unlimited access to the scheduled lineup, all at an incredible discount.
- Staff training programs for audit, tax and preparation, compilation and review
- Certificate programs offering comprehensive curriculums developed by practicing experts to build fundamental core competencies in specialized topics
- National conferences presented by recognized experts
- Affordable AICPA courses on-site at your organization – visit **aicpalearning.org/on-site** for more information.
- Seminars sponsored by your state society and led by top instructors. For a complete list, visit **aicpalearning.org/publicseminar**.

Take control of your career development

The AICPA | CIMA Competency and Learning website at **https://competency.aicpa.org** brings together a variety of learning resources and a self-assessment tool, enabling tracking and reporting of progress toward learning goals.

Visit the AICPA store at cpa2biz.com/CPE to browse our CPE selections.

Governmental audits have never been more challenging.

Are you with a CPA firm or state auditor office? If so, join the Governmental Audit Quality Center and get the support, information and tools you need. Save time. Maximize audit quality. Enhance your practice.

For 10 years, the GAQC has committed to helping firms and state audit organizations (SAOs) achieve the highest quality standards as they perform financial statement audits of government, single audits, HUD audits or other types of compliance audits. If you are not yet a member, consider joining the GAQC to maximize your audit quality and practice success!

Join online today at gaqc.aicpa.org/memberships and start on the path to even greater audit success. Membership starts at just $190 (for firms or SAOs with fewer than 10 CPAs).

Benefits at a glance
The GAQC offers:

- **Email alerts** with audit and regulatory updates

- A dedicated **website (aicpa.org/GAQC)** where you can network with other members

- Access to Resource Centers on Single Audits (both under the new Uniform Guidance for Federal Awards and OMB Circular A-133), *Government Auditing Standards*, HUD topics, GASB Matters and much more

- Audit Practice Tools and Aids (e.g., GASB's new pension standards, internal control documentation tools, schedule of expenditures of federal awards practice aids, Yellow Book independence documentation practice aid, etc.)

- Savings on **professional liability insurance**

- A **website listing** as a firm or SAO committed to quality, which makes your information available to the public and/or potential purchasers of audit services

- Exclusive **webcasts** on timely topics relevant to governmental financial statement audits and compliance audits (optional CPE is available for a small fee, and events are archived online)

Topics the GAQC webcasts cover include:

- Auditor Planning for the New Uniform Guidance for Federal Awards

- GASB Pension Standards

- An Overview of the Latest OMB Compliance Supplement

- Audit Quality Series Avoiding Common Deficiencies

- HUD's Audit Requirements

- Planning Considerations for your Governmental and NPO Audits

- Don't be the last to Know — Fraud in the Governmental Environment

- Yellow Book and Single Audit Fundamentals

To learn more about the Governmental Audit Quality Center, its membership requirements or to apply for membership, visit aicpa.org/GAQC, email us at gaqc@aicpa.org or call us at 202.434.9207.

AICPA® CPExpress

Just-in-time learning at your fingertips 24/7

Where can you get <u>unlimited online access</u> to 900+ credit hours (650+ CPE courses) for one low annual subscription fee?

CPExpress, the AICPA's comprehensive bundle of online continuing professional education courses for CPAs, offers you immediate access to hundreds of one and two-credit hour courses. You can choose from a full spectrum of subject areas and knowledge levels to select the specific topic you need when you need it for just-in-time learning.

Access hundreds of courses for one low annual subscription price!

How can CPExpress help you?

- ✓ Start and finish most CPE courses in as little as 1 to 2 hours with 24/7 access so you can fit CPE into a busy schedule

- ✓ Quickly brush up or get a brief overview on hundreds of topics when you need it

- ✓ Create and customize your personal online course catalog for quick access with hot topics at your fingertips

- ✓ Print CPE certificates on demand to document your training – never miss a CPE reporting deadline!

- ✓ Receive free Quarterly updates – Tax, Accounting & Auditing, SEC, Governmental and Not-For-Profit

Quantity Purchases for Firm or Corporate Accounts

If you have 10 or more employees who require training, the Firm Access option allows you to purchase multiple seats. Plus, you can designate an administrator who will be able to monitor the training progress of each staff member. To learn more about firm access and group pricing, visit aicpalearning.org/cpexpress or call 800.634.6780.

To subscribe, visit **cpa2biz.com/cpexpress**

Why AICPA?

Think of All the Great Reasons to Join the AICPA.

CAREER ADVOCACY SUPPORT
On behalf of the profession and public interest on the federal, state and local level.

PROFESSIONAL & PERSONAL DISCOUNTS
Save on travel, technology, office supplies, shipping and more.

ELEVATE YOUR CAREER
Five specialized credentials and designations (ABV®, CFF®, CITP®, PFS™ and CGMA®) enhance your value to clients and employers.

HELPING THE BEST AND THE BRIGHTEST
AICPA scholarships provide more than $350,000[1] to top accounting students.

GROW YOUR KNOWLEDGE
Discounted CPE on webcasts, self-study or on-demand courses & more than 60 specialized conferences & workshops.

PROFESSIONAL GUIDANCE YOU CAN COUNT ON
Technical hotlines & practice resources, including Ethics Hotline, Business & Industry Resource Center and the Financial Reporting Resource Center.

KEEPING YOU UP TO DATE
With news and publications from respected sources such as the *Journal of Accountancy*.

MAKING MEMBERS HAPPY
We maintain a 94%+ membership renewal rate.

FOUNDED ON INTEGRITY
Representing the profession for more than 125 years.

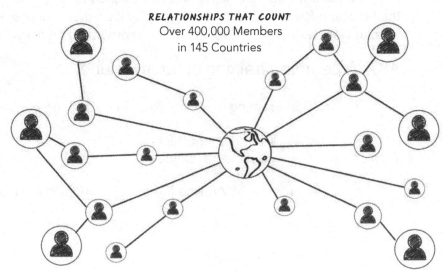

RELATIONSHIPS THAT COUNT
Over 400,000 Members in 145 Countries

TO JOIN, VISIT:
aicpa.org/join or call 888.777.7077.

Printed in the United States
By Bookmasters